Spells

for the Witch in You

By the same author

Spells for Teenage Witches

Spells

for the Witch in You

Marina Baker

KYLE CATHIE LIMITED

This book is dedicated to:

My mother for constantly nurturing my witch. My husband for helping me to
understand the Green Man and our children for showing us how simple life can be.
I salute all our friends for sharing the mystery and joy on the journey of discovery that
led to the writing of this book. I am indebted to Doreen Valiente and Sally Griffyn, for
their honesty, insight and inspiration.

   If you have any questions and want to get in touch with me, you can contact me at
marinabaker@emara.com.

First published in Great Britain in 2001 by
Kyle Cathie Limited
122 Arlington Road
London NW1 7HP
general.enquiries@kyle-cathie.com
www.kylecathie.com

Reprinted 2002

ISBN 1 85626 411 4

Project editor Caroline Taggart
Designed by Mark Buckingham
Text edited by Anne Newman
Photography by Juliet Piddington
Styling by Wendy Deaner
Illlustrations by Abby Hughes (pages 8, 9, 29, 36, 37,
40, 46, 47, 56. 57, 76, 77, 85, 99, 101, 108, 109, 118,
119, 132 and 133) and Mark Buckingham (pages 7, 10,
11, 23, 31, 32/33, 35, 51, 55, 61, 66, 67, 69, 80, 81, 89,
100, 110, 113, 114, 125, 127, 128 and 129)
Production by Lorraine Baird and Sha Huxtable
See also further copyright acknowledgements on
page 143

Marina Baker is hereby identified as the author of this
work in accordance with Section 77 of the Copyright,
Designs and Patents Act 1988.

A Cataloguing in Publication record for this title is
available from the British Library.

Printed in Singapore by Kyodo Printing Co Pte Ltd

Contents

INTRODUCTION

Do you believe wishes can come true? Can prayers be answered? If you suspect it's possible, this book is for you. Or more precisely, for the witch in you. And you probably didn't even realise you had one.

But you do. Through your witch you have inherited the collective wisdom of humanity. For your witch is the voice that calls from deep within, urging you to slow down, be kind, care about others and about our planet.

I can understand you being concerned about harbouring a witch – they've certainly had bad press over the last few hundred years. You may be confusing our witches with the witches of the fairy tales who wear pointy hats and fly around on broomsticks, turning princes into frogs and fattening up children for supper.

Or you may think witches are evil owing to historical reports about men, women, children, even cats being put to death on suspicion of sorcery. Some of them may have had evil intentions, but on the whole it's safe to assume that the majority were innocent victims of a religious fervour coupled with the odd boundary dispute. For if you shopped your neighbour for witchcraft and they were found guilty, you got to take possession of their land. It's not difficult to see why witch hunts caught on big time.

But witches, on the whole, aren't evil. They are generally brave spiritual beings, champions of good causes and the keepers of a simple sacred truth: if we revere nature and live in balance with the world, we can harness the magical forces of the universe and make our desires reality.

That is what spells allow our witches to do. But before you get stuck in, I should warn you that spells don't always go according to plan. You cast a spell, you think it hasn't worked and suddenly something else happens and you realise that you could have worded your aspirations more carefully. Not sure you understand? You will.

To be on the safe side, always ensure your spells adhere to the number one rule of witches: only wish for good. Have your will, so long as it harms none. For whatever magic you cast out into the world may return to you threefold. Basically this means be horrid and three times as much horridness may be heaped upon your head. By the same token, if you wish for good, particularly for others, three times as much goodness may come to you.

Perhaps you still can't quite believe there's a witch in you. That's fine. Cast a few of the spells from the chapter called *Spells for the Voice Within*. In next to no time you'll have a vibrant witch, refreshed from decades of slumber, ready and willing for all sorts of life-enhancing magic. Really, no special gift is required. We are all born with a natural aptitude for witchcraft.

Unfortunately, modern living often works against us, suppressing our witch, our conscience, with the vagaries of 21st-century living. Be patient. Once you begin your search, the witch in you will answer your call, I promise you. My witch has cast a spell especially for you – yes you – to ensure this happens.

Then you'll shine as only someone nurturing their witch can. Your skin will be clear, your eyes will be bright, your hands will be soft and loving and not only that, you'll be happy, too. And when we're happy, there's nothing stopping us spreading the magic of peace and happiness to everyone we meet.

Now where's the harm in that?

Blessed be

Marina

WITCHY

WORKSHOPS

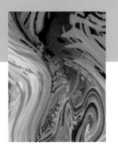

1 God and Goddess

According to legends, the deities of old led extremely complicated lives, to rival any modern soap opera for plot twists and drama. Greek, Roman, Egyptian and Celtic gods, among others, got married, had affairs, occasionally killed each other, brought each other back to life, had drink problems and committed some pretty heinous crimes against the mere mortals who worshipped them.

But within each community of deities, the world over and throughout history, there tends to be one common theme: among a myriad of deities you find a mother Goddess and a father God who together are responsible for life's continuation. These archetypes are what witches refer to as God and Goddess. They have many guises but are most simply symbolised by the sun (God) and the moon (Goddess). When they come together as a couple, they bring about the resurrection of life each spring. Hence Goddess may be symbolised by the earth and God by the Green Man, half human, half foliage, at times her lover and at other times her son.

Since the 18th century, we have become more and more reliant on science to explain all the unexplainable things that we once left to religious doctrine and dogma. There's now, apparently, a general consensus that we no longer need gods at all. Consequently we find ourselves living in a spiritual and moral vacuum. It's as if our relentless march towards something called progress has turned out to be nothing more than the nomadic wanderings of the spiritually dispossessed. But science has yet to provide important answers. In fact, the more we learn, the more we need to know. We understand the mechanics of dying. But what happens to our thoughts when our lungs stop breathing and our hearts stop beating? Do they die with our physical bodies? Or do we continue to exist on another level? Some people believe a Big Bang was responsible for the creation of the universe. But if so, what triggered the bang? Why did our planet go on to develop as it did and how many similar planets are out there?

God and Goddess can't supply these answers. What they can do is help us cope with the unfathomable. They halt the mind from boggling. Look up to the sky, see the moon, see the sun. Look around you at our world. Accept that this is it and make the most of it. So long as it harms none. God and Goddess embody this natural world and provide a much-needed spiritual element in our lives. By welcoming them into our hearts, we acknowledge that within us all is a shared intuitive morality above and beyond the laws of the countries in which we live. Laws may help a country run more efficiently (although not always more democratically), but laws don't make us

all much better people. God and Goddess can, since by their nature they are able to represent unity, respect between the sexes, sexualities, races, nations, cultures, subcultures and generations.

God and Goddess may also be seen to govern (symbolically at least) the laws of nature to which we must all submit. They express a higher truth where "all nature is but art, unknown to thee; all chance, direction which thou canst not see, all discord, harmony not understood; all partial evil, universal good." God and Goddess are the silver lining to the cloud, and they are the cloud itself. They are the forest fire and the life that rises phoenix-like from the ashes. If we respect their domain – our natural world – God and Goddess are kindly, benevolent deities. When we refuse to play by their rules, plagues rain down upon us. If we are to earn their respect we must take only what we need and replace what we can.

When we invoke God and Goddess, we accept implicitly that we are their guests in this world, and well treated we will be if we honour their generosity.

2 The Spirit and the Elements

Old ideas continue to survive for as long as they have resonance. The notion of the four elements makes total sense today, as it has done for thousands of years. Many cultures, from the Chinese to the Native American and including the Celts, the Tibetans and the Japanese, have as part of their belief system, an understanding that our world and everything in it is derived from earth, air, fire and water.

These four elements do cover it. Check it out. Look around you right now. Indoors or out, all that surrounds you is a product of the big four. Bricks? Earth mixed with water, heated to high temperature. That requires fire and the fire requires air. Trees? Water, air, earth and fire (from the sun) all played their part. Without the four elements and the way they balance and interact with each other, there would be no life, or no life as we know it, on our planet. As with all things wiccy (a modern slang term describing anything associated with witchcraft), there is an added spiritual dimension to this perfectly logical (though highly unscientific) way of viewing the world.

Each element is associated with different aspects of personality. Basically, air goes with things like communication, logic and willpower. Earth is about being grounded, home issues, growth etc. Fire covers passion and inspiration, while water is connected with being easy going, or having the courage to change.

Gather together some natural bits and pieces and categorise each under one element. Some will want to appear under two headings, but go for the more obvious. Consider what each object and its respective element suggests to you emotionally. This self-knowledge, carried forth into your spells, will improve things no end. Need firing up? Light a candle. Need cooling down? Hug a crystal.

Spirit is altogether more esoteric than the four elements, despite being known as the fifth. Scientists may well appropriate the word "Spirit" when they get close to understanding the true nature of anti-matter (after all, they nicked "elements" for their basic atomic building blocks). But for now and for witches, Spirit is perceived as an energy, the driving force behind creation, present in all things.

In spells I use the word Akasha in the same context as Spirit. Akasha is an Indian word meaning space or ether. I use Akasha quite simply because I enjoy saying the word out loud. It's softer than Spirit. Plus I like the Indian belief that within Akasha there is a karmic tally for all. So if you cast a bad spell, it will be noted within Akasha, reminding the universe that you're owed a bad time threefold. It's a bit like St Peter's list at the Pearly Gates, or Santa's careful observations on who's been naughty and nice. Akasha certainly keeps me on my karmic toes.

3 Breathing

In order to cast effective spells you need to breathe properly. The rush of oxygen will energise your witch.

Sit on a straight-backed chair – if you try this standing up, you may come over all giddy. Have your feet on the ground with your legs uncrossed and place your hands, palms up on your lap. Close your eyes.

Breathe in through your nose for seven counts, hold for seven counts, breathe out for seven more counts, than breathe out again for a further seven beats.

If you can't manage seven counts, try five or even three to begin with. You will find it easier if you use your muscles to hold out your ribcage for the in-breath and keep it there for the first out-breath. Allow it to lower for the second and contract your solar plexus at the bottom of your ribcage.

On the in-breath, breathe in light. Imagine your lungs filling with a warm energy of golden or amethyst light. Breathe out pain, stiffness, anger, annoying thoughts, darkness, sickness – all your troubles.

Eventually you will begin to feel relaxed although fully conscious and will be able to focus your mind on precise deliberate thoughts. This may take practice. Those who already meditate or do yoga will find it easier.

✝ Tools and ingredients for the witch

The most important ingredient in every spell is you. These days we've come to expect a quick fix for everything. We tend to blame doctors when we can't be cured, our teachers when we fail at maths and anybody but ourselves when we run up debts. Some people are dealt the worst blows in life and often they seem to cope better than others do with a broken finger nail. (I exaggerate slightly, but you know what I mean.)

Basically, we must take responsibility for our lives – even when the misfortune appears outside our control. We must do our best to overcome our problems and put things right as best we can. The key is mental fortitude. This is something that can be developed and is essential when you are casting spells.

The hardware, such as wands and candles, turn what might be just a thought or a wish into a ritual, a spell. They help to take us out of ourselves, removing us from the norm, delivering us to another realm where we may feel the Spirit, tune into the force and allow ourselves to achieve all that we so desire. It's not the wand that is magic, it's you.

It's the same with all the ingredients. It is the understanding of their symbolism and their symbolic use that transforms things like crystals or driftwood into magic spell ingredients.

Always use the most natural things available, from bowls and goblets to wands and pentacles. Choose wood, metal, crystal or glass and avoid plastics like the plague.

Here follow some basic explanations of the tools and ingredients of a witch.

The herb garden

Growing your own plants is essential. Using the fruits of your toil in your spells will improve the outcomes no end. Forced herbs, available from supermarkets, are no good to anyone. Herbs have magical healing properties in their own right and are most helpful when grown with love and attention in your own space.

Whether you have pots or a plot, herbs are the easiest type of plants to grow. They are happy in poor soil and many don't mind how much sun they get, so long as they get some. When it's hot, they will need watering, but don't overdo it. In time and with practice you will discover the fine line between too little and too much.

Cultivate as many of the following basic herbs as possible, according to the space you have.

Lavender	**rue**
rosemary	**mint**
basil	**vervain**
sage	**chives**
chamomile	**pot marigold**
fennel	**lemon balm**
thyme	**bay**

There are plenty more to choose from and an infinite number of books to instruct you.

Harvest most herbs as they come into flower if you plan to dry them. To dry, hang them in bunches from hooks in a dark, well ventilated but draught-free space, such as the airing cupboard. Once they are totally dried out, after about three to five days, store in jars.

Other plants that deserve the attentions of a witch include roses, cornflowers, love-in-a-mist, hollyhocks, foxgloves, forget-me-nots, spring bulbs, nasturtiums and sunflowers, among others.

Ingredients of the elements

Flowers, stones, soil, feathers, incense, liquid, candles may all be used to symbolise and invoke the powers of the elements and of the Spirit. You are limited here only by your imagination and ability to interpret the source of these things.

The beauty of these objects is that they are easily found. Mind you, a stone obtained from a motorway hard shoulder is unlikely to be as effective as a pebble from your favourite beach. But I'll let you be the judge of that. Many of these objects, of course, represent more than one element at a time. Take driftwood. It inclines towards symbolising water and earth, but the original tree from which the wood came also required air and sunlight. When you burn the driftwood, air is essential to create fire. It's a wonderful completed circle of the elements. It is the same with beeswax candles.

The longer you meditate on the symbolism of the elements, the more sense this will make to you. I can only bring you to the gates of wisdom. Pass through and you will understand.

Candles

A beeswax candle, when lit, represents all four elements and the Spirit, just as driftwood does. In spell work candles are just as useful as a light to see by (so much more magical than electric lighting), a purification tool or to seal a spell.

If at all possible, always use pure beeswax candles. Beeswax is a renewable resource and is considered better for your health than paraffin candles (the most common nowadays), since burning beeswax offers relief to asthma sufferers. Paraffin candles, on the other hand, are made from oil and we all know the kind of damage oil (in the hands of humans) has done to the environment.

You should also avoid scented candles (unless you're sure the scent is a pure essential oil) and any with labels that purport them to be "magic" or to "bring peace". At best this is well meaning, at worst it's a blatant rip-off. To be honest, it might be better to use natural undyed beeswax candles and tie a simple silk thread of colour around them in place of any coloured candles suggested in my spells.

Essential oils

So popular have these become that the market is filled with cheap imitations and dilutants. Essential oils have very real healing properties and can greatly influence moods and emotions. That's why it's so essential to use the real thing and get the dosage right. This is nigh on impossible when you don't know precisely what you're using.

A good essential oil comes in a brown bottle and should be described as organic, if possible. Price is another good indicator of the real thing. Oils such as jasmine, neroli, rose and chamomile may seem expensive, but they can last a year (two in a fridge) which makes them much better value than a pair of shoes at 10 times the price.

Generally speaking, oils should not be applied undiluted to the skin. Instead, they should be mixed with a carrier oil, such as sweet almond or wheatgerm, although olive and sunflower oils are also suitable. For every drop of essential oil you should use 2ml of carrier oil. For example, 5 drops of lavender to 10ml of almond oil.

In a bath, never use more than 5 drops of oil and swish around before climbing in.

Book of Shadows

Some of the spells instruct you to make notes. Jotting down your feelings thoughts and observations, sketching and drawing symbols, allows you to express your witch.

Some witches call the notebooks they use their Book of Shadows. Others call them mirror books because they reflect their innermost thoughts.

I like the phrase "Book of Shadows". It suggests that the contents explore the dark recesses of our subconscious, that they provide evidence of the fleeting thoughts we so rarely give ourselves the chance to acknowledge.

Begin your own Book of Shadows. The paper should be plain, undyed and hand made. (But a school exercise book will suffice to start with.) You can press flowers in it, write poetry and tell it all your secrets. A Book of Shadows is one of the most helpful tools available to the witch.

Crystals

Every culture, from Native Americans and Incans to ancient Greeks and Egyptians, has a history of using gemstones in healing or religious ceremonies. The choice of which stones or quartz were used depended on what was available locally, whether it was found in the area or could be obtained by trading.

The ceremonial tools of religious leaders to this dary are encrusted with gemstones. It's not just a show of wealth, it's a historic remnant of a belief in the powers of such stones.

My logical side would say: they're just posh pebbles. But having worked with amethyst I can attest to its peace-promoting, stress-relieving qualities, while my experience of rose quartz is one of emotional healing – it's a stone for both aspects of love.

Both amethyst and rose quartz are simply rock crystal with various minerals present that give each their distinctive hues. Does this scientific explanation make either less special? I don't think so. But judge for yourself.

Crystals come in all sizes and all prices. You don't need enormous great chunks. Nor do you want them polished or carved – a nasty new trend whereby the centre is dug out so that you can place a candle in the middle of it. What is that all about?

Traditionally you are supposed to wait until you are given a crystal, rather than buying it yourself. If you think such considerations will influence the efficacy of your crystal, then go with your instincts. For what is clear about crystal use in spells is that they enable you to harness not just the powers of the universe but also of your mind, which, as I have already said, is the most important ingredient in magic making.

Before using a crystal, cleanse it and charge it up. Do this by first soaking it in clean water for 24 hours, then place it outside for a full moon cycle (28 days) in a position where moonbeams will be able to shine directly on to it. This means not allowing foliage or a building to overshadow it.

The Moon

Our nearest celestial neighbour is more than a decorative feature of the night sky. As old as the earth herself, she has made an outstanding contribution to the development of human culture. Without the moon it is most unlikely that we would be the successful species we are. In humankind's early days, the moon provided a valuable light source for hunting or travelling at night. In Jane Austen's time, grand house parties were still planned around full moons to allow guests to travel after dark. Coastal settlements, whether they realised it or not, were also helped by the moon, since its gravitational pull causes the sea to rise and fall, thereby allowing various foods to be harvested from the shore at low tide, as well as aiding fishermen to get boats in and out of harbours.

But possibly the moon's greatest contribution has been to empower us with a sense of time. Having realised that there was a regularly occurring pattern to the moon's appearance and movement, our ancestors began to plan their farming year around these cycles.

One full wax and wane of the moon gave them a 28-day unit – almost a month. Thirteen of these gave them a year. In addition, they noted that it takes 19 years for the moon to rise and set in precisely the same position. So millennia before the advent of the clock and the Gregorian calendar, humans were able to view time in decades.

Having a concept of such a long length of time must have changed our perception of ourselves. For once you can plan ahead, you can imagine a future. And if you can imagine a future you can imagine a past.

This led to the asking of all the big questions we are still asking today: why are we here? Where did we come from? What's it all about? etc. And so myths and legends were born – practically from loins of the Moon Goddess herself – in every culture of our world. These narratives were more than fireside entertainment to explain the unexplainable. They allowed valuable survival information – an aural farming manual, if you like – to be passed down from generation to generation.

The planning and ordering it gave our lives allowed communities to flourish. We turned away from hunter-gathering and set ourselves up as farmers instead. But it wasn't just the fertility of the land that was governed by the moon. Because our menstrual cycles (and those of our animals) coincided with the moon's cycle, mating could be planned – or avoided, depending on the availability of food. It was the dawning of civilisation as we know it, all thanks to the constant gentle rhythm of the Mother Goddess, our moon.

On a more practical note, witches tend to cast positive action spells on a waxing moon – that is, the period leading up to a full moon. This would be a good time to launch a business venture or a personal project. If you want to stop doing something, or banish a problem, a waning moon – between full and new – is considered best. It's an energy thing, apparently.

Pentacle

This is a five-pointed star retained within a circle. The star itself is known outside the craft as a pentagram. It is the circle that makes it a pentacle, although some witches refer to the symbol as a pentagram and the object on which it is shown as the pentacle.

Confused? So was I. Since I have retained my childhood allergy to maths, I prefer just to use the word "pentacle" whether I'm referring to a round disc with the symbol or just the symbol itself.

Pentacles may be made from metal, stone, clay or wood. To draw the shape, which may then be carved or painted, you will need a pencil and compasses.

First draw a circle. Then place the compasses on the diameter and make a neat cross. Place the compasses on this cross and make another mark on the diameter. Continue all the way around the circle until you have five marks. Join every other cross together and you will then have a five-pointed star within a circle.

With practice you can draw a pentacle in salt, soil or with your hand, with the judgment of your eye, rather than the tools of geometry.

Sage stick

Sage sticks are used in Native American rituals. Burning sage cleanses and purifies a space. An excellent thing to do before all spells, or if you want to work in a neutral atmosphere.

First grow your own sage from root cuttings or seeds. Harvest when you need it. To dry you need a dark space, slightly ventilated but not draughty – an airing cupboard, perhaps. Hang sage from threads in loose bundles. Plants are about 70 per cent water and to dry them completely may take three to five days: when it snaps easily between your fingers, it's dry.

Bunch the sage together and wrap with a thread. When required, burn the end and waft the smoke about. Extinguish and keep for future use.

Wand

You can buy crystal or ornately carved wooden wands. But I would suggest you work with your hands to begin with, just as children finger-paint before taking up a brush. There is enough for the newly acknowledged witch to take on board, without having to worry about where to put your wand – you may find yourself halfway through a spell when your wand knocks your candle over.

You will be requiring a wand at some point. But it is definitely not needed immediately. Don't feel disappointed, though. This is a good thing. I could say, "Get a wand, now, before we go any further. You can't work without a wand." But to me, the wand is the symbol of the witch – along with the cauldron and the broomstick. When you are perfectly comfortable with your witch, you are ready to find your wand.

My current wand (hazel), a gift from my Green Man of a husband, has a snake carved in honeysuckle wrapped around it. Very elaborate. It's also long – more of a stang than a wand. This means that I can lean on it as well as point it. This earths me. My first wand came from a hazel tree in a friend's garden.

When you are ready to find your wand, go to the woods in search of a hazel. Often it looks more like a hedge shrub than a tree. It has lovely long, straight branches. Cut one of these, after asking permission from the Spirit, and then give thanks. You won't harm the hazel. It likes to be coppiced – it thrives on it, in fact.

If you don't know what a hazel looks like, you should find out. But let's be real. A wand doesn't have to be made of hazel. It was the druids who revered it as a sacred tree. Oak, apple, cherry or ash can also be used. Antipodean witches may find eucalyptus just as wand worthy.

The point is, as I have already said, a wand, like all the instruments and ingredients of spells, is a symbolic tool to aid you in your rituals. Modern witchcraft does not amount to a set of proscriptive rules. Quite the opposite is true. All the ideas and beliefs are readily adapted to your lifestyle and environment. Don't allow anyone to tell you otherwise.

5 Colours

Las Vegas notwithstanding, our primary source of light still comes from the sun. Rays beam across our planet in daylight hours, bouncing off all and sundry. When this light shines into our eyes three different kinds of receptors on our retinas respond to the wave length and frequencies, reporting to our brains.

If the waves are short and the frequency low, we see blue. If the waves are longer (although still only about a millionth of a metre long) and the frequency higher, we see red. Somewhere in between, we see green. Three colours, the basic primaries (I love that number three). Combined they create white light. Mixed in twos they create cyan, yellow and magenta. All other hues are infinite variations on the theme. How clever is that?

A less scientific but equally valid approach to colour is to ask yourself, "What's my favourite and why?" Chances are you will have emotional attachment to certain colours because of your personal life experiences. You may also be influenced by how these colours are used to communicate certain ideas, or thoughts.

Red, for example means: "Stop" or "Danger". Notices written in red are designed to alert. Letters written in red are deemed rude. Red also symbolises blood, life and death, as well as love. Green on the other hand is the colour of nature's garb, the environmental movement, seasick faces and of envy.

It's the context in which we view colours as well as their actual tones that determines how we respond to them. So never think that colour is unimportant. What you wear and how you decorate your home will say something to you and to everyone you meet.

In spells, colour affords us several opportunities. We can use it symbolically, evoking the elements, Spirit, God and Goddess. We may also use colour to alter our moods, or as a medium for meditation. Our choice of colour allows us to firm up in our minds what we want to achieve, so long as we can associate our needs with the colours involved.

Various people have produced lists suggesting a magical lore of certain colours. Really what they're saying is, "This is what these colours mean to me." Often these will coincide with traditional associations that through no coincidence reflect the natural colours visible in our world.

The following is a table of my own personal interpretations of colours, from which I choose the coloured ingredients for my spells. Study my chart, then get out into the natural world and see if you can personalise them. Helpful activities include staring up at the sunlight streaming through leaves, gazing at the sea, heath lands, grasslands and your garden at various times of day throughout the changing seasons of the year. Sunsets and sunrises will expose you to more reds, pinks and oranges than you ever knew existed.

Make a note of your observations and feelings in your Book of Shadows (see page 18). This will eventually stand you in good stead for saying, "That Marina should have used orange there." At that point you can say, "Yep, my witch is totally awakened", and begin to develop effective spells of your own.

red	healing, strength, life, vitality
pink	honour, friendship, compassion
orange	to seal a spell, energy, assertiveness, hope, the sun, fire, God
yellow	intellect, communication, self-esteem
light blue	protection, peace, patience, water, air
green	prosperity, good fortune, natural wealth, earth
brown	earth, animals, comfort, security
purple	inner tension, meditation, the colour of the witch, healing, ambition
dark blue	impulsiveness, depression, a need for change, deep thought
dark purple	negativity, change, release, rebirth, confusion, chaos, intuition, God and Goddess
silver	intuition, Goddess, dreams

6 Bonfires

If ever proof were needed that we can harness the magic of the universe, bonfires are it. Dancing around them and cooking on them, deriving warmth and light are absolutely ancient traditions. Using fire is the one activity that marks human beings out among all the other creatures of the animal kingdom.

When man first realised fire's usefulness and utilised that flame, it was possibly the biggest technological breakthrough ever known to humans, radically changing our way of life even more than the motor car or the worldwide web. We could live without those, but we could never relinquish fire.

Fire, of course, is an energy. When you burn wood or coal, the energy a tree derived from the sun and from water is transmuted. It becomes light and heat.

This energy has great virtue. It can purify: before picking a splinter out of your finger with a needle, you can pass it through a flame to kill all germs. Fire also regenerates: wood ash makes a great fertiliser for soil; following a forest fire, renewed life thrives on it.

Witches thrive around fire for all these reasons. (Even though it was once tradition to burn them on huge pyres – strange, that. Would it not have been more apt to bury them alive, depriving them of the elements altogether, instead of sending them off painfully but paganly, at one with Akasha?)

Fire is the greatest nurturer for all those witches who have grown stiff through years of being ignored. It's the real biggy of all the elements. It's the sun, it lights the moon and it had a hand in the creation of everything. If you can, you should have a fire pit in your garden and an open hearth in your home.

Anything less is a compromise, unless you head out into the countryside. This shouldn't be attempted by novices though, since you don't want to go setting fire to large tracts of the countryside or woodland, do you? See the rules of bonfires on page 28.

How to create a fire

For outdoor fires, you first need to create a fire pit, around 1m/3ft in diameter and 25cm/10in deep. Whether working outside or indoors with a fireplace, the rules of fire lighting remain the same.

You need to build a mound, slightly pyramidal in shape. At the bottom place dry grass or screwed up newspaper. Above this place small twigs or inch-thick pieces of wood. On top of this gently place larger pieces of wood and a few logs, or coal. Light the paper or grass. If it appears to be having trouble getting going, blow gently, until the kindling "takes". You won't need any lighter fuels.

When it's time to replenish the wood or coal, be careful not to disturb the "heart of the fire" since this will make everything burn faster for a few minutes before burning out.

Indoors, if you have a grate that can be opened or closed, keep it open when lighting up (to create an up draft) and close when the fire is roaring to allow it to burn more slowly and last longer. If you need help with your up draft, take a large piece of newspaper and cover the fire place opening for about 20 seconds. Call it serendipity, but you really do get a better class of fire from a broadsheet. Be careful not to set light to the paper.

What witches use fires for

Fires are considered a must for gatherings and sabbats (see pages 133-142) as well as more private moments when casting spells. When organising a gathering you will need a large grill, which is easy enough to come by, especially in the summer months. This will enable you to cook upon your fire. Male witches are particularly enamoured by such a ritual.

If you have a cauldron, you can cook soups and stews – well, honestly, what did you think a cauldron was for? Okay, spells occasionally, but essentially cauldrons are for cooking in.

I am aware that, indoors, an open fire is, in the modern age, considered an architectural luxury. If your home doesn't have a chimney, let alone an open hearth, a candle will symbolise all the life-giving qualities of the flame. Many people don't even have gardens, so again, work with candles whenever a fire may be required.

But in terms of communing with your witch, nothing beats an open fire for an evening of contemplation or spell work, either alone or with family and friends. A real fire also has health benefits. A chimney opening provides ventilation. It doesn't clog a room with fumes as gas fires seem to, or give off a dry, asthma-inducing heat like central heating.

Another wonderful thing about fires is that they are all different and some are easier to light than others. So experiment. Getting to know your own fire and local fuels (some burn better than others – wood should be seasoned and dry) is a great process of discovery in itself. You will come to love, I hope, the ritual of fire building and take pride in improving your ability to provide yourself and all who visit your home with a "right roaster".

Rules of the fire

1) Avoid liquid fuels and fire lighters altogether. They're unnatural, smell awful and make food taste funny.

2) Try to burn wood or mix wood with coal. Coal is a non-renewable resource. Also, check that your log supplier doesn't just vandalise woodlands and orchards to make a quick buck.

3) All children must be supervised.

4) Always have your chimney swept if you haven't lit a fire there before.

5) Sweep chimneys once a year.

6) Once a chimney has been swept, especially in spring, light regular fires to deter birds from nesting.

7) Consult with your local authorities about what fuels may be burned in your area. Cities are often smoke-free zones.

8) Don't light a whacking great fire in the garden in daylight hours if your neighbour's got a washing line full of laundry. On a warm evening, check the wind direction and strength. You don't want to upset anybody with your smoke.

9) Don't dig a fire pit too close to a tree – you may set fire to its roots!

10) In the countryside, never light fires when conditions are dry, never build a fire upwind of crops, and always dig a pit and or surround the fire with stones. Make sure you have water or sand standing by in case of an emergency. Don't leave the fire smouldering. Respect private property.

7 Sacred sites

We've all heard of Stonehenge. Many of us have heard of Avebury and Newgrange. But there are stone circles and ancient monuments scattered all over the world. Are these places any more magical than the herb garden in your local park?

Maybe, but maybe not. Sacred sites are special because for thousands of years people have gathered there to worship, to celebrate life or to be healed. Some people believe that these sites echo with the intensity of the feelings felt there, compounded by the number of people involved.

But a site is most sacred because it is sacred to you. My garden is definitely sacred, as are the Standing Stones on Cape Clear Island (West Cork, Republic of Ireland) where my husband and I were married.

Should you choose to cast spells at recognised sacred sites, prepare to share the Spirit with a bus-load of tourists filming the occasion. But don't let that put you off visiting; just try to go early in the morning or in the evening when holiday makers are busy eating.

For more privacy, check out sacred sites marked on ordnance survey maps, respect countryside lores to get to them and never leave candles burning.

Alternatively, go to a quiet beach (one without ice-cream vendors or funfairs), an ancient woodland (not a recently planted pine kitchen factory), or climb a hill or the foothills of a mountain.

Taking time out to place ourselves within natural surroundings can have the most uplifting effect and is something many of us don't do often enough. As my mother always said as we yomped across fields, fighting off cattle to reach a stone circle: "If you want to choose your own path, you have to get off the beaten one."

This, and a mistrust of cows, has stayed with me in adulthood and is something I shall pass on to my own children, once they've grown a bit and can run when I tell them to.

8 Children

Because of their natural curiosity towards the world, children are often more in tune with their witch than their parents are, and will thoroughly enjoy casting some of the more activity-based spells in this book under your guidance.

Children are also most receptive to the general lifestyle of the witch. Since they know no other way and are eager to learn, they will happily embrace a way of life that reveres nature and respects the individual needs of all people, so long as they are set a good example.

But kids should also be advised that magic is not a simple alternative to self-discipline and hard work. If they want to achieve their maximum potential, magic can help, but they must also apply themselves to the rigours of modern life. Help them to understand that the world is not perfect but that they can contribute to improving it for their own well-being and that of future generations.

To nurture the witch in your children ensure they get a healthy diet of home-cooked food with lots of fresh vegetables and fruit. Avoid over exposing them to junk food and television, as these are known witch suppressants.

Provide plenty of learning experiences for them, from walks in the woods to creative play. Sing with them, play music with them. Talk to them. Fairy tales are a great source of wisdom, told in the traditional manner – around a fire.

9 Good witch practice

Whatever it is that you personally seek from witchcraft, be it the wisdom to put your troubles into perspective, the courage to face your problems head on, or a wild card to change your hand of destiny, never lose sight of the fact that you as an individual are part of a greater whole. Everything is connected, even if we do choose to ignore this fact for the sake of habit or convenience.

"Have your will, so long as it harms none." That's the witches' motto, or wiccan rede as it is also called. For as every witch will discover, whenever you cast a spell, the results may return three-fold. Excellent news for those seeking to increase their own and other people's happiness. Bad news for anyone with selfish, spiteful or downright no-good motives.

But it's not just when casting spells that we can play lip service to the rede. It should permeate every aspect of our lives. Unfortunately nurturing our witch in this way goes against the genetically modified grain of modern living.

Nearly every routine, from commuting to cooking, can have a profoundly negative effect on the state of the planet and the state of ourselves. The following lifestyle tips may seem obvious. And they are. But sometimes we need reminding that a healthy lifestyle and an enormous respect for our natural resources are the key to a happier life. For too long human beings appear to have thought otherwise.

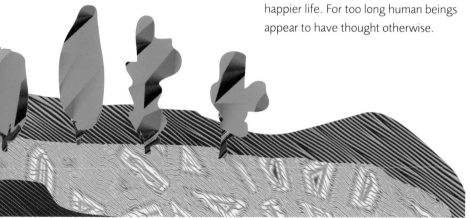

Exercise

Exercise daily. You'll be more instinctual, alive to new ideas and you'll sleep better. Swimming, cycling, dancing and walking are great. Yoga, Pilates and Alexander technique can also be beneficial – but not if you zoom down the pub directly after a class.

Healthy eating

Where possible eat fresh, locally grown, organic produce. Fruit, vegetables, protein and wholemeal carbohydrates should all be eaten on a daily basis. Vary your diet – rotate the colours of fruit and veg and explore new protein sources to ensure a good balance of essential minerals and vitamins.

Drinking, smoking and drugs

No lectures, no demonising. But we all know the health score. See the helpful spells on pages 63-69.

Green issues

Recycle everything that can be recycled: paper, plastics, cans, tins, glass. Avoid using plastic bags – use cloth ones instead. Dispose of uncooked kitchen waste in a compost bin.

Walk, ride a bike or use public transport if you can.

In the home, insulate your roof and windows, turn your heating down a few degrees, wash laundry at 40°C (100°F). Heat only as much water as you immediately need in a kettle. Turn the thermostat down on your hot water tank and add less cold to your bath. Better still take showers instead.

Buy electricity from a company using renewable energy sources. Governments are beginning to realise that more effort is needed to explore wind, water and solar power. But we probably won't be able to produce enough for current demands. It is down to us as individuals to cut down on the energy we use. We have to change our habits. Fewer baths, more showers. Less tumble drying, more line drying. More jumpers, fewer radiators. Many of the spells in this book involve a bath, granted. But that is because a bath in itself should be seen as a ritual, something unusual, and not an everyday occurrence. A bath involves a lot of energy in its creation. Use this energy to help you cut down on consumption elsewhere in your life.

Support local eco-friendly businesses, from organic food producers to log suppliers, furniture manufacturers and candle makers. It may cost more money but it won't cost the earth.

Gardening

Californian researchers have discovered that gardening reduces stress levels. All witches know this anyway, but it's always nice when science catches up. A well-tended herb garden or vegetable plot also provides an invaluable source of nutrients, healing properties, fragrance, colour and interest for the mind, body and spirit.

Gardening is not that difficult and a knowledge of food production is something all humans should have. If it is left as

the preserve of a few industrialised profit-driven individuals we will no longer have control over how our land is farmed or what we're given to eat.

Your garden should be free from chemicals, and brimming with life, animal, vegetable and mineral.

Politics

Know what's going on in your community, your country and the world at large. Turn out to vote at national, county, state and local levels.

If something really gets your goat, take it up with your local representative, join a pressure group or start one.

Dancing

Dance. It's so good for the soul. Outside, barefoot around a fire is best (so long as the ground's not littered with holly leaves or other forms of spikiness), but all forms of dance allow us to commune with our own spirit and the Spirit.

SPELLS

FOR THE

VOICE WITHIN

The voice within is the voice of your witch. These spells will lead to greater success with all other spells.

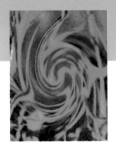

Wisdom

This perfectly simple spell will bring joy, spiritual nourishment and welcome changes…if you let it. It's certainly helped my family and friends. See page 27 for advice on building a fire.

Throw the salt and lavender on to the fire and sit back.

Focus your gaze beyond the flames and you will begin to see images. Ask yourself what these mean to you, in the same way that you'd try to interpret your

an open fire • salt • lavender • flowers

When the flames have died back, take the salt and lavender in your hand. Tell yourself what you'd like an answer to.

dreams. Meditate on the images reflecting your innermost thoughts.

Self-esteem Goddess spell

When you can't find a suitable mate, or your career seems to be in the doldrums, it is all too easy to allow your self-esteem to plummet. As a result, your ambitions appear as ever more distant dreams.

You have to believe in yourself before you can believe in anything else. This spell is the first step to reclaiming your confidence and liking yourself once

more. It's an ongoing spell, which means it may be repeated for as long as it's needed. But don't do the bath bit more than once a week. Casting a spell should be a special occasion. Cast them too often and they become nothing more than obsessive behaviour. There's a fine line between that and ritual behaviour. Try not to cross it.

Run the bath to a depth and temperature of your liking. Put the lavender oil and oak leaves into it, swish it around. Light the candles and climb in.

Close your eyes (but don't fall asleep). Begin the breathing exercise on page 13. Breathe in a warming orange

When you leave the bath, snuff out the candles and thread the oak leaves on to the purple thread. Then, whenever your self-esteem fails you, heat jasmine oil in a burner, light the candles, hold up the oak leaves and repeat the chant.

a bath • 7 green oak leaves (or bay leaves if these are out of season) • lavender oil • a purple candle • a yellow candle • jasmine oil • purple thread

light of confidence. Breathe out murky coloured self doubts.

Imagine a yellow light above your head which slides down your body, touching every bit of you from the top of your head to the tips of your toes. Continue to breathe in slowly through your nose and out through your mouth. Say out loud, "I am gorgeous. I am beautiful. I am Goddess." Repeat six more times.

When the leaves eventually run out, begin again with new oak leaves and candles.

The oak leaves may be carried with you (in a small box or envelope) in your handbag on (all sorts of) important dates. When touching up your make-up, just whip them out and repeat the mantra to spur you on to greater things.

Altar to Akasha

It need not be flash and it certainly doesn't want to be reminiscent of a high church altar. But somewhere in your home or in your garden you can create an altar to the Spirit on a shelf, small table or large stone.

It will contain representations of the

stones • crystals • feathers • shells • candles • vases of flowers • driftwood • carved or clay pentacles • a wand • an oil burner

four elements, Spirit, God and Goddess. Your altar also serves as a reminder of your more spiritual moments that brought you wisdom and insight as to the true nature of yourself.

You can add to your altar as and when you desire, change it with the seasons or clear it and start again. However you wish.

The items listed above may be varied to your own tastes and resources.

When no other spell seems to quite serve your purpose, or you won't give your witch the chance to be heard, light three candles on your altar (you choose the colours, but the chart of symbolic colours on page 25 may help you), heat up your favourite oil and say, "Give me strength to cope Akasha, I can't do it alone." Follow this with a conversation with your witch discussing the issues to hand.

Once you've formulated some sort of resolve, say, "Thank you Akasha for making your presence felt and for helping me to better understand myself. Blessed be." Trace the sign of the pentacle in the air with your hand or wand if your prefer.

Mountain spell

For seemingly insurmountable problems, you must learn to behave like the wind that goes over or around the mountain.

the mountain pushing you up or sideways. Enjoy the feeling.

Return to your problem. Ask yourself,

salt • 5 blue candles • a notebook

If you choose to go over, ensure you have time to admire the view from the top.

Sprinkle the salt to create a large pentacle on the floor. Place a candle on each point. Sit in the middle of the star, close your eyes and breathe (see page 13).

Imagine you are the wind, a forceful power. Now visualise a huge mountain in your path. Choose which way to go. Feel

can you change the problem by finding alternatives to just ignoring it? Do you need to rise above it? A clue may reside with the direction you chose, as the wind, to blow.

Mull over ideas for sorting out this issue as you go to sleep. First thing when you awake in the morning, write down your thoughts or dreams. Your solution rests here.

New Moon resolution

When you are working hard to change a particular aspect of your life, give yourself a boost at the time of a new

a dark purple candle • white thread

moon. Reaffirm your conviction or promise with this simple spell.

Wrap the thread around the candle about a third of the way down. Light the candle and begin your breathing (see page 13). Stare into the aura emanating from the flame. Say to yourself, "Great Goddess, attune me to the energies of the newly waxing moon. Diminish my bane by the time she must wane. I am committed to this change, though weak at times. But success will be mine with careful thought and strength of mind. It is my will. So will it be. Blessed be."

Summer rain

A good spell for allowing you to experience natural energies with your six senses. Yes, six. Use all five and the sixth follows. This spell also allows us to heal – ourselves and others. It needn't be a sickness, it may be that you and a friend or relative have fallen out.

Wearing just light, indoor clothing go outside when it is raining. Hold up your hands and face to the rain. Feel it, listen to it, taste it, smell the changing fragrance. Experience your tensions being washed away as the water drips down your body.

Breathing as instructed on page 13, breathe in pale green hues and breathe out darkness. As you become energised send healing energy out through your hands. Send this to someone who might benefit. Imagine the force moving from raindrop to raindrop until it reaches them.

When you feel they have been'
touched, go to a tree and give it a hug
(but not if there's lightning and the tree
ground via your feet. For a moment you
may feel at one with the tree. Don't laugh
until you've tried it. If you have total

a tree • rain

stands alone in a field). The tree has also
benefited from the summer rain. Absorb
some of this positivity and allow it to
travel through your body and into the
privacy, this is a good spell to try naked,
but that isn't strictly necessary. Just don't
wear waterproofs, as they will create a
barrier between you and the rain.

You're innocent when you dream

For this spell, also known as the Destiny spell, you first need a vision. So long as your choice of vision respects you, others and the planet, go for it. Your future is what you make it. This spell might be the beginning of great things.

You decide.

When you have finished the apple, take it outside and bury the pips and the core if you haven't consumed it. When it's gone, say: "This day I have read my thoughts and will act upon them." Point

a silver candle• a mirror• an apple• a wand

Nothing is certain until dreams become plans of action. Hence, you're innocent when you dream. Light the candle and look in the mirror. Breathe properly until you can determine which thoughts you want to be having and which are superfluous to your present needs.

Bite into the apple as you watch yourself. Don't look away. Keep facing you. That niggle, the thought that keeps flashing through your mind, is that the one, the big one? What is this thought saying? Is it urging you to stop something or start something?

your wand towards the moon and trace an arc down to the ground where the apple lies, saying, "I draw strength from the Goddess who understands the cavernous mysteries of the soul. May I look to her to charge my destiny that I may achieve my goal. And may the God that lights her body in the sky reflect also my desire, may my enthusiasm burn with this life-giving fire. I will have my will. And so will it be."

Keep a notebook by your bed. During the night or when you wake up, write down all the thoughts related to your destiny. Then act upon them.

Initiation

A confirmation and welcome rite for your witch. Don't feel you must cast this spell before you can begin on others. This is a life. Give thanks for the times when you could have chosen a different route but didn't.

**an apple log • a bucket of brine • an open hearth •
3 silver candles • white, yellow and blue flower petals • a drop of cumin oil •
a drop of benzoin oil • a drop of amber resin oil**

spell for when you come to recognise the benefits of expressing your witch and want to make a promise to yourself to allow your witch to flourish.

Soak the apple log in brine for a moon cycle, beginning on a waxing moon. If you can't get hold of seawater use a packet of good-quality sea salt with fresh water – from a spring if possible. Dry out the log before attempting this spell on the night before a full moon. Place the three candles on the mantelpiece. Light your fire according to the instructions on page 27. Use wood rather than coal. When it is well lit, heat your oil.

Light your candles and place the log on the fire. Sprinkle the petals in a semi-circle from hearth to hearth and sit within it, cross-legged. Begin your breathing.

Think about the path you took to arrive at this auspicious moment in your

When you arrive back in the now, say: "Great mother, great father, God and Goddess. I acknowledge your presence and the beauty you bring to this world. From this day I shall live by the witches' rede. I shall have my will so long as it harms none. I may make mistakes. I may stray from the path. But may I always find a welcome return in my heart and accept that what's done is done.

"Help me to heal and to nurture kindness. Give me the wisdom to know when to talk and when to listen. Allow me to recognise love and give me the determination to create happiness and the power to pass on this gift to others. I ask this in your honour, Great Father, Great Mother. I do this for me and all others. So let it be."

Should your fire burn with a blue flame you are blessed indeed.

SPELLS FOR FRIENDS AND FAMILY

The spells in this chapter address

just some of the issues involving

close relationships other than those

with lovers. Those in other sections,

however, such as Health or Practical

Magic, may well be just as relevant.

Friendship spell

Giving is one of the greatest sources of spiritual well-being. Don't wait for birthdays. Give to someone who is ill or suffering a career or family setback, or to a person who has helped you in some way.

This spell is guaranteed to make

scent, colour and availability. Obviously if you grow your own, that's even better!

In the week leading up to a full moon, leave the crystal and quartz outside to charge. Put the jasmine in the basket and if it's mature enough, weave the tendrils around the basket handle.

a basket with a handle just a little bit bigger than the plant pot
• a jasmine plant • 3 spiral sea shells • an amethyst crystal
• a piece of rose quartz

anybody feel special. Jasmine naturally flowers in the spring. I chose it because the scent is so uplifting. At any other time of year you may prefer to choose a different plant. Base your decision on

Place the sea shells, quartz and crystal on the soil, saying, "I call on the Spirit to bless this gift and bring joy to the receiver."

Spell for three friends

When three friends put their witches together, magic returns 27-fold. This is a good spell for commanding healing for outcomes. This will help you to word your desires carefully.

When you reach your joint decision,

a bonfire
• 3 pieces of apple branch

someone, or to launch a joint project, be it your own company, good works for charity or to bless a party.

Get your bonfire going (see page 27). When it's roaring, stand together holding hands. Breathe in golden healing light and breathe out your bane.

Pick up your wood and between you discuss what you'd like to change. This may take some time and you'll probably need to vote on it. Be wary of what you do wish for, bearing in mind your magic will come back threefold times three times three. Discuss all possible

point your apple wood towards the fire with each tip touching and say: "Together we can bring about positive changes." Each express your wish in your own words. Then say: "We have the will and have harnessed the power of the Spirit. The God and Goddess will receive our dreams and know our hearts to be pure. If it be their will as it is ours, so will it be. Blessed be."

Throw your wood on to the fire and take a few moments to absorb the implications of your actions and to give thanks.

Family squabbles

Children, teenagers, siblings, parents, grandparents. Family members have more in common than we like to admit. But all too often we focus on the differences. Knowing which button to press is easy when you've inherited the same buttons. Instead of respecting each

Twist the hairs together by rubbing them between your fingers. Attach to the thread using the same method. Carefully tie on to the candle about a third of the way down.

Light the candle. Mix the petals and strew them to create a pentagram (see

a hair from each family member's head
• red thread • a light blue candle
• blood-red rose petals

other's opinions we fall out sometimes over trivia and occasionally over big things like reaching puberty.

Life is bumpy enough. Kin should stick together to ease each other's ride. This spell will help to bring harmonious understanding to family relationships, even to quarrelling siblings. Don't burn bridges, build them.

If you're not talking to one or all of the relatives in question, you will have to go and visit. Snaffle the hair secretly – they probably won't understand what you're trying to do.

page 22) with the candle in the centre. As you do this say: "The same blood courses through our veins. Though times change this remains the same. May the power of the Spirit forge our hearts, allowing us to express and to receive the love of kinship.

When the candle burns down through the thread, the spell is cast. Go and visit whoever it is that you have been quarrelling with. Take them a single rose as a gift. You could, alternatively, incorporate the rose into a tussie mussie (see page 120).

Nursery amulet

The image of a hand, be it painted, sculpted or wrought from metal has, for millennia, been used to ward off evils. This version, using the hand prints of you and your family, will not only offer press flat on the paper. Use a separate piece for each person. These may be framed if you like, then hung between a child's bed and the windows or the door.

If you have the patience and

sky blue paint
- **coloured paper of your choice (see colour chart page 25).**

protection, it's fun to do and continue to do as little hands grow.

If working with a newborn baby you may have to wait a few days or weeks until their fingers naturally uncurl and the hand is flat enough for printing purposes. If you like, you can start with just the parents' and older siblings' prints and keep adding.

Sponge the paint on to the hands, then

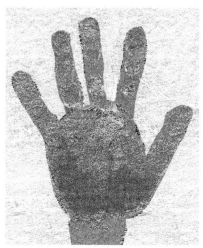

determination, you could print enough hands for a decorative frieze. It goes without saying that this hands-on spell works best when you create in the right frame of mind. Ask God and Goddess or Spirit to bless your work and to protect your family from all the unknown and unforeseeable disasters that might befall you.

Nursery nightmare talisman

From toddlerdom onwards children may begin to suffer from nightmares. There needn't be any very significant underlying cause for this. Events such as

Alternatively make up the following nightmare talisman to catch your nightmares and attract good fortune and sweet dreams. Get kids involved with

a walnut-sized stone with natural holes
• 4 spiral sea shells, each with natural holes • sky blue thread
• 2 pieces of driftwood each about 25cm/10 in long

starting at nursery, or moving house may contribute. But so does the development of vocabulary, memory and imagination. Children can begin to put words to their fears, to see shapes in shadows. What was once the rustle of trees becomes the movement of monsters.

In America, it has long been a tradition to hang "dream catchers" over the bed. Their recent increase in popularity among non-native Americans means there's a deluge of kits and models to buy consisting of plastic hoops and beads and feathers of unknown origin. Far better to make your own with clay or glass beads, wooden hoops and feathers you collect yourself.

the gathering of materials and the making of the talisman, explaining that this will protect them.

Form a cross with the two pieces of wood and bind together with thread. Tie a piece of thread through the stone and attach the other end to the centre of the wooden cross. Thread the shells and attach one to each end of the wood. Add extra thread to the centre for hanging.

As you hang it up, with the child present, chant together: "Go away nightmares. We're not afraid. The sweetest dreams shall take your place."

Don't hang it directly above the pillow. Either place it at the foot end of the bed, or a couple of feet along from where they rest their head. This is for two practical reasons. Firstly you don't want it falling on them. Secondly, it could be distracting and might prevent them from sleeping soundly, compounding the problem of nightmares.

Sweet dreams.

Sound sleep spell for children

Allow the child to sit up in bed with the lights off or low and the curtains open. Let them point their wand skywards, night family, good night all, I shall not stir 'til morning's call."

The parent or carer then closes the

a wand

• a warm comfortable bed

saying, "Up above the world so high I gaze upon the night-time sky and call upon the stars in space to sprinkle magic sleep dust on my face. Good curtains, saying, "Snuggle down and close your eyes, no more peeps, it's time to sleep." Remove the wand for safe-keeping.

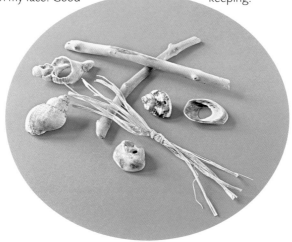

Yes Do

Does your CD seem to be sticking? Does every sentence addressed to your child begin with the words "Don't" or "No"? Chances are kids don't even hear this. They probably think it's one of those meaningless words like "Hey" or "Now".

bright yellow paper

• purple paint • orange paint • glue glitter

• a hair from every head in the family

I'm sure you have very rational reasons for using negative terminology. But turn the issue on its head. Instead of saying, "Don't swing the cat by its tail dear," try, "Can we put the cat down now and come and listen to a story?"

I know. You're at your wits' end. But if you carry on down this path, you might fall off your wits altogether and that's not going to help anybody. This spell will allow you all to draw a line under this

problem and renew your family bonds.

If the children are young, you paint the words Yes and Do all over the paper with the paints. Older kids can have a go on their own.

This being magic, patience is required. Allow the paint to dry before continuing.

Read a book, play in the garden or bake some bread together while you wait (see Bread Spell, page 120)

Splatter the glue over the paper, add the glitter and hair and help the child to say, "Don't say don't, please say do. I promise I'll be good for you." Mummy or Daddy says, "Yes, yes, yes, I know I should. I'll be good if you will too."

Pin the spell up where you can all see it and be reminded of your promises.

Walk away

A night out with the girls can get pretty messy but the worst you'd expect is tears before bedtime. Boys, on the happily coupled men choose sandalwood or frankincense. Single men out on the pull may be over-

2 drops of one of the oils mentioned here
• 2 drops of bergamot • 5 blue candles • some light food (including bread)

other hand, can be very dark. One beer too many and some males of the species (though by no means not all) are spoiling for a fight. I've experienced this first hand and it can be very frightening.

Many a gentleman may find himself embroiled in a situation not of his making. What normally happens is that a group of louts pick on someone less threatening than themselves or are sexually suggestive to a woman without realising that the giant standing next to her is her lover and a brute to boot. The next thing you know, furniture and fists are flying.

This spell is designed to exert a calming influence on men preparing for a male bonding session. Choosing the right essential oil for this spell rather depends on the men in question. For

stimulated by the aphrodisiac qualities of these potions. They would benefit from something more calming such as pine or orange. In a mixed group of men, opt for the latter.

Use your charms to lure the men (your friends) to your home. Just before they arrive, wipe the oil over the candles, place them in a circle and draw a pentagram between them with your finger (see page 22). Light the candles one by one, saying, "By the power of the four elements, earth [light the first candle], water [light the second, etc], fire and air, and by the Spirit may these men be protected. May Akasha bless them and keep them calm should any forces threaten harm."

Hand round the food (eating before drinking always helps), and wish them joy as they head out on their adventure.

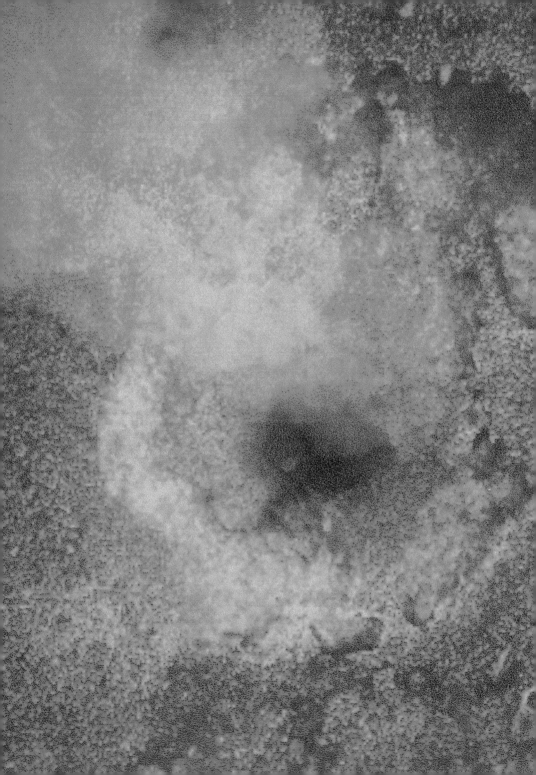

SPELLS

FOR

HEALTH

We all have an innate ability to heal

ourselves and others. We just have

to attune ourselves to the Spirit and

believe in what we're doing. The

spells in this chapter will help.

Driftwood spell

The sick person need not be present at this healing rite. It is to help you and friends tune in to your healing capabilities. We can all do it, I promise you.

This spell may be performed in a garden or on a beach, at night,

Dance or walk around the fire slowly in a clockwise direction, while staring into the flames. If you're new to witchcraft, you might find this embarrassing. But try it. You might be amazed. A chant may come to you.

kindling (twigs and paper) • dry driftwood
• 5ml patchouli oil • 5ml cedar oil • a suitable place to light a fire

preferably on the night of a full moon, or in the two days leading up to that point. You may work alone, or with like-minded friends or relatives. Don't force anyone to join in against their will, since their negative feelings will affect the way that you and others work – you won't be as relaxed as you could be. And the more relaxed you are, the less self-conscious and more successful you will be.

Pour the oil on to the driftwood, allowing it to soak in for up to half an hour. Choose one piece of driftwood, to represent the sick person and hold it back while you use the kindling and the rest of the driftwood to light your fire.

Something along the lines of: "Fire, fill me [us] with your strength to heal. Fire allow me [us] to heal." It should be short and something you can say over and over. If you are incorporating this spell at a sabbat, there may be references to the time of year within a healing context.

At Imbolg you might add, "May the power of the Goddess in all her forms nurture our sick friend." At Yule you might add, "It is the time of rebirth, the returning of the light. Cernussos shine on [person's name] and heal their plight."

When you are ready (you will know when this is), take the driftwood and hold it up to the moon saying, "Goddess, [person's name] is sick. We call on you to help them. Please soothe their pain in the healing fire."

Light the driftwood with flames from the fire and hold it up to the moon once more, saying, "In the flame their pain will burn as Akasha fights their bane."

Place the wood on the fire saying: "Thank you Akasha for empowering us to heal."

Hold your hands out to the flames and feel the heat and might of the Spirit entering you, lending its healing powers.

Self-healing spell

For all sorts of ailments from strange viruses to back pain and rotten colds. A healthy diet and appropriate exercise will strengthen your constitution. This spell, taught to me by my kind friend and healer, Ruth Farber Nathan, will help further. It is also helpful for emotional complaints from anger to a broken heart.

Heat your oils on a burner. Sit on a comfortable chair or sit up in bed and

they merge. Feel the energy of the Spirit. It spirals down through the top of your head bathing you with its healing powers. Your bane is carried from the centre of your body on the upward spiral out through the top of your head.

This endeavour can take a bit of practice. Persevere. Once you are in charge of your spirals, continue to

a drop of eucalyptus oil • 2 drops of lavender oil

begin your breathing exercise (see page 13). With your eyes closed envisage a clockwise spiral of golden light in front of you. When you can "see it" envisage another spiral, this time moving in an anti-clockwise direction, next to it.

Draw the spirals towards you and towards each other so that you and

explore the experience for as long as your concentration allows. Throughout you should continue breathing as explained on page 13.

When you can no longer sustain your spirals, say, "I am healing, I will continue to heal. Thank you, Spirit."

Hands-on healing, preparing for the worst

A severely ill patient may well have their body pumped with all sorts of prescription drugs or chemicals. Never apply essential oils to their skin since this could lead to uncomfortable and unnecessary side effects. Instead, oils should therefore be heated on a burner and allowed to waft.

Your healing may lead to a miraculous recovery, but chances are it won't,

feel ready to allow your healing energies to flow. You may become aware of a tingling sensation; the hairs may stand up on the back of your neck. When you feel prepared say, "We breathe in golden healing light. We breathe out our bane." On your in-breaths the air you take in is flecked with gold. As you breathe out feel dark energies leaving your body. Do this seven times.

oil burner • 3 drops of lavender oil • 2 drops of geranium or jasmine oil

especially when tried as a last resort. This is no reason not to offer healing. It can ease a person's pain, infusing them with positive energies, helping them – and you – to prepare for their passing over.

Hold the patient's hands. Allow them to rest in a comfortable position as best they can. Both of you close your eyes. Begin with the breathing exercise on page 13.

Breathe like this for as long as it takes for you to

Then say (having learned it off by heart), "I call on the almighty Spirit in all things to help us in our hour of need. The power of the universe flows through us, between us, within us, bringing light and hope, diminishing darkness and bane. May [person's name] be healed."

Keep breathing until you begin to sense the charge of energy. Place your hands on the patient's face saying, "The Spirit is here to heal you. Be healed by this power."

The Change

Physical symptoms coupled with mental anxiety can make the menopause a difficult and sometimes traumatic ordeal. Do your best to view this singular life-changing event in a positive light. When your hormones calm down so will your emotions. Hopefully you will then come to realise that this transitory period, this

ice cubes and place them around the wheat and hips.

Carefully kneel (you can use a cushion to make it more comfortable) and then lean forward with your hands on the ground outside the petals to embrace the circle. Sit back and watch the ice cubes melt. Trace your hand

**2 ears of wheat • a sprig of rose-hips or hawthorn berries •
lavender • sand • red petals or in autumn, red leaves • 7 ice cubes •
7 sprigs of broom bound with an orange ribbon • a bowl**

rite of passage, marks your emergence as a wise woman. You will be able to draw on your life's experience to offer kind wisdom and advice to the younger sisters who have yet to reach the potential of their elders.

This spell was given to me by my mother, now a beautifully wise grandmother, thoroughly enjoying the fruits of her age.

Outside on the grass lay down the wheat, crossing the stems, and place the hips or berries on top. Sprinkle with lavender. Pour the sand in a circle and the petals around this. Take the

around the circle in an anti-clockwise spiral, signifying rebirth.

Say, "Hot, cold, pleasures, sorrows merge. Tension eases, the circle flows. I welcome my tomorrows when my bane will be gone. I will heal, I will be wise, I will smile anon."

When the ice cubes have melted, sweep up all the ingredients and place them in a bowl. Scatter them on a flower border saying,: "I was the maiden, I was the mother. I am now the wise woman. May my symptoms dissolve and my wisdom flourish."

Potion for the Change

Pour 3 drops of chamomile or fennel oil into your bath and swish around before you climb in. These same herbs, dried, may be drunk as a tea to soothe your symptoms.

Magic throat potion

Perfect for coughs and sniffles. A calm night's sleep practically guaranteed.

minutes. Add the honey and stir until dissolved. Top up with cold and serve

an organic chamomile tea bag • a teaspoonful of organic honey • ½ cup of hot water • a dash of cold water

If symptoms worsen or persist, however, especially with a small child, consult a doctor to rule out asthma, croup and more serious childhood diseases.

Steep the bag in hot water for five with the words: "This is magic throat potion. It will make you feel better and help you to sleep. It's magic, yes, it is. Take a sip and see."

Backache

Continuous backache should be investigated by someone in the medical profession. Speak to your doctor and don't let him/her palm you off with painkillers, although occasionally these will do the trick for more short-term problems. But then so will this spell.

An awful lot of back pain is due to bad posture, both sitting and standing, and/or stress. Even if you have been diagnosed with a specific problem, from rheumatism to a misalignment of the spine, the stress and pain caused by your condition will exacerbate the problem. Backache is another cause of...er...backache.

Try this potion to ease your pains and woes away. Pour it in a bath and soak yourself; heat it on a burner; or mix with 10ml of sweet almond or olive oil and

2 drops of lavender oil • a drop of rosemary or clary sage oil • a drop of ginger oil

There also seems to be an association between an aching lower back and a troubled heart. This doesn't necessarily mean a turbulent love life. It could just as easily be a sense of unfulfilled or missed potential.

get a friend to gently – very gently – massage it in to the affected area.

Whichever method you choose, accompany it with the breathing exercise on page 13. Breathe in a pink healing light. Breathe out your bane.

A spell for over-reliance on alcohol and other unhelpful habits

Drinking helps us to relax and makes us slightly braver than we might otherwise be. We can easily become overly reliant on these effects. It isn't that drinking is all "bad", it's just that we miss out on so much when we're half cut all the time.

Do you always drink when you get home from work or when the kids go to bed? This is symbolic drinking to mark the watershed between "your time" and "my time". Yet a relaxing soak in the bath

or an invigorating (and environmentally more friendly) shower, coupled with a spell represents a highly effective alternative.

Maybe you drink because you're thirsty, dehydrated from too much coffee. Could you possibly drink a glass of water between top-ups?

Some of us can't enjoy a party unless we're off our heads dancing on tables. Why not opt for better music that will

63

get you dancing anyway? Or how about trying the Goddess spell for self-esteem (page 38). Or even the humbleness spell (page 117), which may help you to realise that it is the empty vessel that makes the most noise.

For anyone with health and emotional problems (related to alcohol or

name. When you next see them, present them with the crystal. Be tactful when you explain why you're giving it to them.

Cast this spell outside, in a place that has meaning to you, where you know you will be able to work without disturbance.

Place the candles in a triangle. Sit

an amethyst crystal • a small orange candle • a small purple candle • a small red candle • glass jars for the candles • a goblet of wine

otherwise), drinking may help you to forget while you're drunk, but it won't help you to heal.

Anyone with a serious drinking habit should seek independent help and advice. But, if it's more a case of a habitual consumption because you haven't thought of anything better to do with your body and mind, try this spell. It will also work wonders for any form of self-abuse from taking drugs to comfort-eating unhealthy snacks.

You can also cast this spell for someone whose behaviour concerns you. Adjust the chants to incorporate their

cross-legged within it with the orange candle ahead of you, the others to each side. Put the goblet down in front of you and hold the crystal in your hands.

It goes without saying that you should be stone cold sober to cast this spell (as with all spells). Begin with the breathing exercise (page 13). As you begin to feel energised, channel your positive feelings into the crystal on your in breaths.

Say, "I feel the healing energies entering this stone. I recognise the sensations of this force and will find them again in times of need when I touch the stone."

Put the crystal down on the ground and pick up the goblet. Take a sip from it then say, "This wine I offer as a sacrifice to the God and Goddess. They give freely of themselves to provide such gifts. I give freely of myself to honour their gifts. I will no longer abuse their kindness. I will no longer abuse myself."

Pour wine around in a circle outside the candles. "I give to Mother Earth and the Green Man as they give to me."

Pick up the crystal and say: "My needs and the Spirit's are as one. Respect and balance will see this deed done."

Whenever you feel yourself slipping back into your old ways, hold the crystal and meditate on the positive effects you felt when first performing the spell. Then go and get a soft drink (organic fruit juice, water or herbal tea).

Warding off the weed demons 1

The weed demons are clever little buggers. They trap you in a hall of mirrors where every sensible thought concerning health and wealth is deflected and boomerangs back as a suggestion to light up. How do those demons do that?

There's no simple solution to casting them out for good. It takes constant vigilance over years, but it must be worth it. You and your witch will flourish without a smoking habit.

Remember: you were not put on this planet to amuse those demons or keep tobacco-industry insiders in swimming pools and Rolls Royces. Reclaim your life. Blessed be! I hope you can make

Up to 3 large cockle or oyster shells

these spells work.

Gather together every ashtray in the house and give them away to a charity shop. If you're scared you'll be tempted to buy them back, throw them off a cliff.

Use the shells in place of ashtrays and say to them, "You beautiful shells don't deserve to be used in this way. I'll feel bad every time I stub out a cigarette on you. I'm so sorry. I will stop."

Every time you flick your ash, or stub out, remember those words.

Warding off the weed demons 2

Stop smoking in one month

Week 1: on one side of the paper draw up seven columns, one for each day of the week. Down the side, write the hours from around the time of your first cigarette of the day, to

along with the pencil and secure with the rubber band.

Every time you desire a cigarette, unwrap your chart make a mark at the appropriate time and day. You should soon see a pattern developing. Make notes

a piece of paper just large enough to wrap around your cigarette packet or tobacco pouch (covering the packet protects you from the auto-suggestive stuff, inherent in the design)
• a rubber band to secure it • a small pencil •
a dedicated note book (not your Book of Shadows – see page 18) •
an enormous amount of witch power

the last one at night.

On the other side, draw the following runic symbols: Death (also meaning new beginnings, illustrated above), War (right) and Disordered thoughts (opposite top).

Wrap the paper around your cigarettes (runic symbols facing outwards),

in your notebook concerning why you smoked five cigarettes in an hour on Monday morning but actually didn't smoke any on Wednesday afternoon. Or whatever.

Week 2: change your brand of cigarettes. Retain last week's wrap but on a new piece of paper draw up the same chart. On the other side draw the symbols for Possessions and Poison (also meaning harmful attitudes and baneful habits).

Keep noting down each cigarette on your chart and exploring the nature of your habit in your notebook.

Week 3: change to another brand of cigarettes. Draw an anti-clockwise spiral and the runic symbols of Love, Home and Wealth (second, third and fourth illustrations on this page respectively) on the chart, with the same calendar on the back. Continue to smoke but not in those circumstances that seem to form the core of your smoking habit. Instead, after a meal, go and clean your teeth. While on the phone, stand up, or move your chair away from your desk. When you're stressed, go for a short walk or chat to a non-smoker.

Week 4: bury your ashtrays in the garden. Prior to going to bed, smoke your last cigarette (any brand but not your old "favourite"). Don't drink, don't talk on the phone or do anything that you associate with lighting up. Just sit there doing nothing except smoking. Any remaining cigarettes or tobacco should then be flushed down the toilet before you go to sleep. The next day go out and spend the money you'd use for tobacco in a week on something for you. A plant, some flowers, a book, an essential oil, a candle or a new lipstick. You choose. Drink plenty of fresh organic fruit juice and water to flush out the toxins.

Congratulations on completing this spell. You are now officially a non-smoker. You haven't "given up" smoking, you have stopped.

Warding off the weed demons 3

To be cast after a week of absolutely no cigarettes (or anything else. No pipes, no joints, no cigars or cheroots).

In your own time say a prayer along the following lines: "I thank the Spirit, I thank myself for releasing me from the

a candle • vervain (lemon verbena) oil • your charts from the previous spell • a silver-coloured platter (cover a plate with foil, if necessary)

Choose a candle of a colour compatible with your current state of mind. For spiritual fortification, purple. To loosen you up, blue. Improving levels of enthusiasm, orange. For intellectual affirmation that you are doing an incredible thing, yellow.

Choose the symbol that meant the most to you, in spell two. Carve it on to the side of the candle.

Wipe oil on the candle with your finger (Oh joy of joys: you no longer have to worry about it making your cigarettes taste funny afterwards).

Light the candle and as you gaze at the flame's aura (don't stare directly into the flame, it's bad for your eyes), allow yourself to feel fantastic about getting this far.

demons. They may try to return. But all their efforts shall be spurned, through vigilance, love and self-belief. I look deep within and find I have the strength to heal and protect myself. No outside forces shall interfere with my determination to continue on this exhilarating journey of discovery as a happy confident non-smoker."

Take up your charts and burn them by your candle. Scatter the ashes outside.

Keep this candle and light it again whenever you feel or hear the demons trying to scrabble their way back in. On a piece of paper write down why you chased them away in the first place and how great you feel as a non-smoker. If you don't feel great, write that down. Then light it by your candle.

Repeat as
often as needed or
desired. Should you be overcome
by those wretched demons, even just once,
you may have to return to the first spell. So
don't let them in.

A pain in the month

Period pain or dysmenorrhoea is exacerbated by stress. This potion

Either pour into bath, swish it around and climb in, or mix with 10ml of sweet

**2 drops of rosemary oil •
2 drops of lavender oil • a drop of clary sage oil**

works wonders so long as there's no underlying medical cause for your symptoms. Speak to your doctor if you're brought to your knees every month or if the pain is accompanied by an upset tummy and/or vomiting.

almond oil and massage it on to your stomach, hips and lower back. The breathing exercise on page 13 will also help. Breathe in pink healing light. Breathe out dark red pain.

Let's make babies

Some women only have to look at their partner and they conceive. For others trying for a baby involves years of false hopes and disappointments with no success at the end of it.

If you are experiencing problems (say after a year of actively trying for a baby) speak to your doctor who will normally arrange a sperm count first, prior to checking the woman for things like pelvic inflammatory disease and

hormonal deficiencies. But it could simply be a weight issue. Overweight and underweight women are less likely to ovulate than their more average weighted sisters. Or it might be age: many women concentrate on their careers in their twenties and early thirties, but by 35 their fertile potential is dropping fast.

Often women younger than 35 would like children but can't find a man. If that's the case, try the Loneliness or Self-esteem Goddess spells (see pages 78 and 38). Try not to be tempted to go it alone as a single parent – it's hard enough work with two adults sharing the load.

Sometimes no cause can be found for infertility. If this is the case consider Chinese medicine with a reputable practitioner. Some of the results, now well documented, are nothing short of miraculous.

drinking or taking drugs – prescriptive or otherwise.

First charge the crystal by placing it outside for a minimum of three days and nights on a waxing moon.

Prepare the candles together, saying, "This may be the day when we conceive, if it is meant to be so will it be. We trust in Akasha to guide our destinies, may we be at one with the life-giving energies."

The woman should run a warm bath. When it is filled pour in the oils and

for the woman
a handful of white rose petals • 2 drops of melissa oil
• 2 drops of geranium oil • a drop of rose oil
for the man
the same essential oils mixed with 10ml of sweet almond oil
for both
2 purple candles wiped with lavender oil • an amethyst crystal

In general, however, the surest way to get pregnant is to stop worrying about it. You've heard of people who jump through hoops to adopt a child only to conceive naturally the moment they bring the child home, haven't you? Well dwell on that before casting this spell.

It goes without saying surely that both of you should be eating well, getting plenty of exercise and not smoking,

swish around before scattering the rose petals on the surface. Climb in, lie back and relax. (It is better for the man not to bathe as it warms up the scrotum and kills off sperm.)

When the woman is ready to come out, the man should light the candles, placing one each side of the bed, the rug or the sofa – or wherever you plan to conduct your love-making. The room should be warm and there should be no other lighting. The man should then collect the woman from the bathroom and bring her into the candle-lit room. Kneel down, naked, facing each other, pick up the crystal and hold it together, looking into each other's eyes. One says, "I love you." The other says, "I love you too." Together they say, "Through this crystal we feel the presence of the Green Man and the Goddess, absorbing their fertility through the supreme energies of Akasha. If it be our destiny to conceive, so will it be. It will be." The man should then lie down while the woman massages the oils into his back or chest, taking as long as you both like. The more foreplay involved, the more chance you have of attaining a simultaneous orgasm which will help your cause further.

Birth spell

This spell is for the first few hours of labour. If you can still talk and walk, clean the cooker and hold a conversation, you before embarking on your journey to the hospital or a preferred room in your home, and motherhood. It will ease the

**3 bay leaves • 3 drops of lavender oil
a bunch of fresh chervil (or tablespoon of dried) • a bunch of mint
• 5 candles – one each of purple (for instinctual guidance), blue (to offer
protection to mother and child), red (to aid the healing process), yellow (for
intelligent decision making) and orange (to seal the spell)**

probably have a while to go and it's the perfect time to take half an hour for yourself – with maybe a partner or friend ready to massage wherever you need it – pain, relax and inspire you, helping you to prepare for this momentous occasion.

So long as labour pains are 20 minutes apart and not becoming more frequent by the minute, you can cast this spell even if your waters have broken, so long as you're still at home. A hospital bath poses risks of infection. Avoid at all costs.

Run the bath deep but not too hot. Light the candles, strew the ingredients on the water, swish them around then climb in. Begin your breathing exercises. Then talk to your child. Say, "Mummy's here. I'll help you, little one. We're together and soon we'll meet. You are protected by Spirit, God and Goddess. They will guide us on this day when we welcome you, little one, to our world."

Keep breathing during contractions. Blow away the pain on your out breaths.

Witches prefer home births. If it is your first child you may be persuaded to go into hospital. But read up on the subject. I believe one of the reasons many people experience long difficult births is that they don't allow their witch to help. Witches make great midwives because birth is the most sacred of all events and witches revere the sacred.

See page 143 for books that may help you to come to an informed decision.

Cures and potions for mother and baby

Child-free readers might feel I focus too much on the the the mother/child relationship compared to other areas that may be alleviated with a witches' brew.

But this may apply to you one day and you may have friends to whom you can pass on the wisdom. It was only when I became a mother myself that I realised how far removed from the natural world the act of child-rearing had become. If we can't allow our instincts and herbs to play a role, instead of leaving it to so-called experts and the drug companies, what hope is there, really, for humanity?

Morning sickness solution

Suck, sniff or smell a lemon. Even thinking lemons, imagining the taste and smell can help. Other than that, take breakfast in bed (eat first, drink later), go for a walk, avoid heavy traffic fumes and cooking smells. And get plenty of rest.

Labour pain compress

Pour a few drops of clary sage oil into a bowl of very hot water (or ice cold if you prefer). Wet the flannel and press hard on the pubic bone as often as needed.

Bringing in the breast milk

Put 2 teaspoons of caraway seeds in a cup with 250ml of hot water. Steep for 10 minutes and strain before drinking. This should be made three times a day (by Daddy, preferably) and always be drunk fresh. You can start drinking caraway infusion safely during labour.

Mastitis

Better than a cure, avoid it altogether. When breast feeding you may feel hot spots or lumps developing. These should be gently massaged at every feed to ease away the blockage which may lead to mastitis.

Soak yourself and your breasts in a hot bath. If you've had a caesarean and the wound is fresh, use a hot compress (a flannel soaked in very hot water with a few drops of lavender oil) on your breasts instead. As you lie there, gently massage the hot red areas. Whatever you do, don't stop feeding from the affected breast as this will make things worse.

If you begin to feel feverish, get into bed (with your baby) and stay there for 24 hours. Apply a hot compress, as above, to the affected area both between and during feeds.

If you start to feel any worse at any point, call your health visitor, midwife or doctor. They may wish to prescribe – and you may well need – antibiotics. Hopefully you will have stopped it coming to this. Drink plenty of fluids, such as chamomile or fennel tea.

Nappy rash

Wipe breast milk over the affected area as often as you like. If possible use washable nappies (which allow the skin to breath better than disposables) and leave them off for around half an hour after a change. Place a towelling nappy over your lap and sit baby on it to avoid messy accidents.

Colic

Some babies scream every night (normally beginning around 7pm) with colic. No amount of rocking or singing seems to help, but I'm sure it does.

Mummy should drink an infusion of fennel seeds. Place 2 teaspoons of seeds with 250ml of hot water. Steep for 10 minutes before straining. Drink three times a day.

SPELLS

FOR

SORROW

Even in your darkest hour may the

light of hope continue to shine.

Trust that the intensity of your

sorrow will diminish with time.

Meanwhile, these spells will help

you cope.

Loneliness

Surrounding yourself with crowds of happy people has one effect on loneliness: it makes it worse. Whatever contributed to your sense of loneliness, the bottom line is that you feel unappreciated and unloved.

ritual, helping you to realise your desire for greater understanding of your situation.

Pour a few drops of oil on to the candle. Light it, then sit cross-legged in front of it. Begin your breathing (see

a tealight candle in a jar
• Vervain (lemon verbena oil) • a sacred place

You may be yearning for somebody to talk to. And yet what is there to say out loud if we cannot treasure "the rhythmic silence of contentment when quiet thoughts replace shared conversation," as my mother puts it.

So open your heart to the beauty of the natural world, listen out for the response of your voice within. This will enable you to find the peace and love that will dispel your loneliness.

Your chosen place may be an ancient monument of standing stones, a beach at sunset, a forest glade, or even your back garden. What matters is that it is sacred to you, giving weight to your

page 13). Breathe in the Spirit of the place. Breathe out your melancholia. When you begin to feel uplifted open your eyes and look around you as if for the first time. Study the sky, the landscape and how one influences the other. Look out for birds and plants. Smell the place, taste it, hear it, feel it on your face, with your hands. Then experience it all with your sixth sense.

Speak to the witch in you, saying, "I am here in the now, I find solace in the beauty of the Spirit, the true meaning of happiness and the futility of loneliness. I shall carry this moment away with me. Whenever my thoughts rest on this time,

I will feel and will be most truly blessed."

Before you return to your everyday world, seek out a memento, perhaps a stone, a shell, or a flower. Take it home and add it to your altar to Akasha or create one (see page 40).

Loss of a pet

The grief arising from the loss of a pet can be overwhelming. You miss their company so much. You may have spent more hours with them than any human being, even a partner. When their time comes to pass on, everyone assumes you'll be okay, because it can't be as bad losing a human family member or a friend. But such assumptions are no comfort at all when you know you'd do practically anything to turn back the clock and have that damp nose nuzzling into you, or their warmth on your lap. As well as their antics, you miss the purity of

talk to your pet. Their spirit will still be there.

This spell is to help your heart to heal while celebrating the joy your pet brought to you. This joy, like their Spirit, will last for ever. When your heart has healed you will be able to relive the joy every time you think of your much-loved, much-missed companion.

Light the candles and hold the token. If you are working as a family, you can take it in turns to hold the token and speak. "Dearest [name of pet], I/we send love and blessings." In your own

3 brown candles wiped with rosemary oil
• a token of your pet such as a toy or a collar

their unconditional love.

Give yourself time to grieve. Have a good cry, get the photograph albums out, talk about your pet. If children are also grieving, they will find this most helpful. If you can bear it, visit your old favourite haunts and

words, send a special message. It may be a reminder of a memorable adventure, or you may fill him in about events since he passed on.

When everyone present has had a turn, one or all of you say: "[Pet's name], though we can't see you, we may hear

you in the wind, in the lapping of the waves, we may feel you in the warmth of a fire, and in the life that springs from the earth beneath our feet. You live with the Spirit and within our memory. Be at peace as we may be. Blessed be."

Funeral wreath

A wreath is symbolic. It represents the circle of life from birth to death. By laying it on a grave you are saying, "I accept that this is natural, however intolerable it may feel." It is also a token of remembrance and respect.

The activity of making a wreath can help you to come to terms with the dreadfulness of your loved one being gone from our physical world. It is also more personal than something purchased in a rush on the way to the crematorium or graveyard.

Bend the wire into a circle and bind the moss on to it with the raffia. Insert the flowers and herbs, tucking them under the raffia or using wire. If you wish to add a card, make one. On one side draw an anti-clockwise spiral (signalling rebirth), on the other, a personal note.

When you lay down your wreath you will know what to say.

wire • raffia • moss • rosemary • rue • flowers and herbs

A living memorial

Celebrate a life with life. Plant this in memory of someone you miss, now that they've passed on.

Clear a circular space about 1m/3ft in diameter in a garden border. In the middle of the circle plant the rosemary and surround it with seashells. Plant sage around the outside of the shells,

When you have completed the memorial say: "Through the changing seasons, may I take comfort from this newly flourishing life and celebrate the passing of a much loved life that meant so much to me."

The calendula may self-seed or need to be replanted each autumn. As the

a rosemary bush • sage • a mix of winter-flowering cyclamen, snowdrops, narcissus and muscari bulbs • calendula (pot marigold, dwarf variety) • seashells • beach pebbles

interspersed with the bulbs. Plant a single circular row of calendula around this. Make a border with the pebbles.

As you work, think about the difference they made to your life, the happiness and fond memories they gave to you, alive in your heart for ever.

rosemary grows you may wish to expand the memorial or replant some of the sage and bulbs as they reproduce (see page 143 for a helpful gardening book).

The death of a child

No parent expects to outlive their offspring. Grief and despair are tinged with a sense of failure. The desire to protect a child is our most profound instinct, yet you have been unable to fulfil this basic need. You are dealt an unfathomable blow and no one can really understand how this feels.

Allow your anguish to ease eventually, rather than allowing it to destroy you completely. And believe me it can. Take as long as you need. My heart travels with yours.

After the death, mix the oil with lamp oil and place in the lamp. Light the flame and keep it burning in a safe place until

an oil lamp • 5 blue candles • yellow rose petals • rosemary oil • bergamot oil • an oil burner

Such a loss is something you may never get over whether your child died in the womb, at birth, in childhood or in adulthood. This was your baby. And now they're gone. The silence, the loneliness, the regret, it's too much to bear.

Years after their death you will still be moved to tears, gulping the uncontrollable sobs that only a parent can express from the source of their soul. Cry you must. This and time are the great healers, although in the first few weeks and months you may not believe it.

after the funeral (it will require top-ups). Extinguish it before you leave for the funeral. You may have to steal yourself to do this.

When you wish to draw strength to cope with this awfulness, sprinkle the rose petals in a circle and place the candles within it. Heat some more oil.

Say nothing. Do nothing except think. Breathing (as described on page 13) will help you to control your emotions. Think about your child, your fondest memory and allow yourself to smile. Their spirit may have joined the

Spirit, but their presence is felt in remembrance. The life that came from you will always be with you. Small comfort this may be, but all the same there is comfort here.

Forgiving the unforgivable

For victims of physical violence or mental torture, be it from a partner, neighbour, so-called friend or stranger. The energy wasted on hating or on constantly fearing another onslaught is better utilised in restoring your self-confidence someone at a victim support group. Your local telephone directory should have suitable numbers, or you could ask at a police station. Witchcraft cannot solve every ill, but it can give you the strength to help yourself.

a bonfire • several shells with mother-of-pearl linings, such as oyster or abalone • rose petals • frankincense oil • clary sage oil • lavender • a pink candle • 2 black candles • paper • a pen • a silver plate or tray

and forgetting it ever happened. Get the problem out of your head and out of your life.

For those colluding in a violent relationship, this spell won't actually protect you from attacks but it should lessen the aggressor's hold over you, giving you the strength to get the hell out of there today. Ignore their protests of true love and empty promises about how it will never happen again. (They've said that before, haven't they?) You may find it helpful to talk to

On the night of a full moon, light a fire, either outside or in your hearth. Scatter the shells and rose petals on the tray and pour on a few drops of frankincense, rosemary and clary sage oil. Wipe lavender on to the candles before placing them in holders on the tray. Light the candles.

Raise your arms into the air, as if drawing up the light from the candles. Say, "I, [your name], call on the God and Goddess to protect me from [aggressor's name] and to act on my

behalf. Should words or actions be used against me, return them to [aggressor's name]'s hearth where he/ she must face his/her own foul deeds embellished by the power of three."

On the paper, using the ink, write a list of emotions and actions you wish to be rid of, such as fear and regret. Don't write the aggressor's name but do include emotions that relate to their actions, such as anger or misunderstanding.

Go to your fire and throw the paper on to it saying, "I am protected, I forgive, I am strong, I am free," seven times. When the candles have burned down, throw the ends, the petals, and shells on to the fire, repeating the mantra beginning "I am protected," a further seven times. Now move on.

SPELLS

FOR THE

HOME

Neighbourhood watch schemes may scoff at the idea of protecting your home by spiritual means. But it does work. You still have to lock your doors, though.

Home peace spell

This may be performed at your home or a friend's, when you've just moved in or if for any reason the occupants are feeling insecure, perhaps because of a burglary, accident or illness. This is a great spell for children to take part in.

Put the salt and lavender in a bowl frequently used communal room and say, "We thank the Spirit for answering our call for health, happiness and harmony. We ask for this blessing in the knowledge that health, happiness and harmony may bring peace to our home. Bring peace, bring peace, bring peace."

a bowl • 3 tablespoons of sea salt • 3 tablespoons of lavender • a red candle

and stir three times with your wand. Go to your front door and sprinkle some of the mixture on to the doorstep saying, "We call on the Spirit to bless this home with health, happiness and harmony." Go to your back door if you have one and repeat.Light the candle in the most

Keep the remaining salt and lavender mixture. Whenever you have an unfortunate visitor repeat the spell - after they've left, of course. If you've just moved in, as friends come to view your new home, invite them to sprinkle the mix and chant the first half of this spell.

Home protection talisman

There is a fine line between protection and fortification. Locks and doors should be solid and windows secure. But you must also be able to escape in an unthinkable situation, such as a house fire. Window bars are excellent at keeping people out, but they can also imprison.

Whatever crime prevention measures you do undertake, ensure the whole household knows planned escape routes and where to locate keys easily, even in a smoke-filled room. Give yourself and your

Melt the wax in a bowl over a saucepan of water. Remove the wicks. Allow wax to cool for about 20 minutes, stirring in the lavender oil and dried herbs before it becomes too solid.

Roll the wax into balls about the size of large walnuts and pierce through with a skewer. When they are totally cooled, thread with the ribbon and attach to the willow arranged in the vase.

As you work, channel positive protective energies into your hands so that these may be worked into the wax.

a large glass or crystal vase • 3 branches of corkscrew willow • white wax from 3 large beeswax candles • 7 drops of lavender oil dried lavender, chives and mint • blue silk ribbon.

family or housemates a fighting chance by fitting smoke alarms with working batteries. Smoke alarms save lives.

Only when you have taken care of the practical can you consider more esoteric approaches to protection, such as this spell.

To help you do this try saying: "I work my magic with wax and herbs to bind all evils to my will. When seen by those who would displease me 'twill change their minds. They'll turn and flee."

Place on a windowsill that you consider vulnerable.

Intruder deterrent

Practical magic at its simplest. If your garden is big enough to support a hedge without the removal of half your lawn, plant hawthorn and holly along your boundaries or under windows, particularly those that tend to get left open such as the bathroom.

You may cut a few hawthorn blossoms for your Beltane celebrations (see page 138) and deck your home with holly for Yule (page 136).

Do-it-yourself spell

Successful DIY relies on doing the work. Yourself. It sounds obvious, yet many of us still live on building sites or move home before the shelves make it to the attack the job with vigour but no expertise. You'll soon wish you'd never started. The Humbleness spell (see page 117) may help you to realise your

a crystal • a yellow candle
• bergamot oil • an oil burner

walls.

Once you have all the tools and materials needed for the job, try this self-motivation spell. It is just as effective for women as it is for men. Just make sure that whoever is undertaking the job knows what they're doing. It isn't enough simply to envisage a newly tiled bathroom then

limitations and call in the professionals when necessary. This might cost more, but it's worth it in the long run. Ask friends for personal recommendations to avoid employing cowboys, or only reliable ones, at least.

Leave your crystal to be charged for seven days prior to a full moon then bring it indoors. Yes you do have to wait for a full moon – you've waited long enough, so what's the big deal?), bring it inside.

Cast the spell in the area requiring home improvement. Light the candle, turn off the lights and heat the oil on a burner. Begin your breathing (see page 13). Make sure the room is well ventilated – you don't want to inhale paint, glue or other chemical fumes.

Once you are focused, get up (slowly) and stand with your legs apart and slightly bent with feet facing forward. You should feel balanced, comfortable and relaxed. Hold a tool, symbolic of the job, in your right hand (or the left if you're left-handed) and the crystal in the other. Continue with your breathing.

Then say, "I call upon the magnificent energies of the universe. With your help, great Spirit, my dithering will be gone. Inspire me to take on this task that so long has been avoided. Stay with me until it is complete. It needs to be done. It will be done. Bless my work, bless me, blessed be."

More often than not, asking your partner to cast this spell will be enough to get them reaching for the tool box.

Home potions

Moth repellent

An orange pomander will keep the moths at bay and is great a gift for all ages to make.

Tie any old ribbon around an orange as you would when gift wrapping so that you have a cross at both "ends". Pin it to keep it in place. Cover the rest of the orange with cloves – you can get as fancy as your patience permits in terms of patterns. Roll the orange in ground cinnamon bark and Orris root, both readily available from herbalists. Store in an airing cupboard until dried out.

Remove the marker ribbon and add a fresh ribbon in the colour of your choice.

Hang the pomander in your wardrobe or give away.

Insect repellent

Grow basil on a kitchen windowsill to deter flies.

Anti-bacterial wipe

For toilets, work surfaces and floors. Use seven stalks of lavender per cup of cold water. Bring to the boil in a saucepan with a lid and simmer for ten minutes. Use a clean cloth to wipe it around your home. Don't store any of the liquid. Instead make it up fresh on the day you're planning to use it.

SPELLS

FOR

LOVERS

Some people say they don't believe

in magic, though they do believe in

love. But to me, love is magic. It

certainly makes us act and feel as

though we're under a spell.

Faithfulness spell

This spell acts as an affirmation between two people in love. It could also be used when making up after a row, especially

Hold it out to each other and kiss it. Whoever instigated the spell should hand their twig to their partner who will

a twig of bay leaves

• **a hair from your head** • **a hair from your partner's head** • **a red ribbon**

one that exposed an element of jealousy, perhaps brought on by a sense of insecurity.

Split the twig in half down the middle. Kneel in front of each other, each of you holding half the twig between your hands, which should be in the prayer position. Hold it up to your lips and kiss it.

bind the bay together using the instigator's hair, saying, "This hair binds us together, neither shall stray, our love is protected with this bay." They shall hand it over to their partner who shall wrap the other hair around it, repeating the charm.

Tie with a red ribbon and hang it up somewhere visible.

Temptation spell

Affairs "happen" for all manner of reasons. Possibly it is because you find your current relationship unfulfilling. Is this because of communication problems or lack of a decent sex life? These two go hand in hand and there are spells in this book to help with both (see pages 94 and 97). Or perhaps you are single and lonely and in desperation are prepared to settle for less than you deserve.

Sprinkle the lavender and salt to form a large pentacle (a pentagram within a circle). Place the candles on each point of the star. Imagine a square around the circle with a straight line running perpendicular to the top point. In each corner place a pebble, a feather, a seashell and a flower.

Sit within the pentacle, facing towards the top point. Begin your breathing (see page 13). Say the

salt • lavender • 5 dark purple candles • 4 pebbles • 4 feathers • 4 seashells • 4 orange flowers

So who is the object of your desire? Are they single, in a relationship or married? Affairs with married people are the biggest no-no that I know of. They invariably lead to heart-ache for all manner of people. It really isn't worth getting involved.

Seek out someone you can trust and talk about it. Often by letting in the light, the temptation diminishes because you can at last see the situation for what it really is – a non-starter in a constant quest for happiness.

following and mean it: "I call to Akasha, the great Spirit, to save me from myself. Open my eyes to the dangers I face. Help me to realise the misery I may cause if I continue on this dangerous course. Let your light shine and banish my bane. Protect all involved from my destructive pain. Lead me away from the misery that awaits. Teach me to love a better way."

Avoid meeting the person who tempts you for at least a moon cycle.

Sensual spell

"I just wish he was around more and would clean the bathroom occasionally or maybe even pick his own pants up off the floor."

Such complaints are commonplace among married couples and live-in lovers. If we cast a spell to banish bathroom and underwear problems, we'd find other niggles to express dissatisfaction like hating their jokes or television viewing habits (actually that's a good one to moan about – try the spell on page 126). The underlying cause of such grievances is usually one of lifestyle. We're constantly prised apart by work and family commitments, and stress, financial issues and other niggling problems add to the confusion.

Overcome these and the bathroom and underpants syndrome melts away. Either your partner will try harder to please you, or, being amply compensated by love and attention, you will learn to live with their foibles.

First you must persuade your partner to join in – this spell only works if both of you are involved. Top hint: you don't

a handful of lavender • petals from 3 red roses • 3 sprigs of rosemary • 6 purple candles (3 for the bathroom, 3 for the bedroom) • a drop of ylang ylang • 2 drops of sandalwood • 2 drops of bergamot

actually have to tell them it's magic. Just lure them into that bathroom and yep, *you* will have to clean it first!

Pack the kids off to a sleepover if you have any and you can. Ensure the bathroom and bedroom are warm. Put clean sheets and pillow cases on the bed. Place the candles safely around the bedroom. Don't light them yet.

Stand naked at the foot of the bed. Sprinkle most of the lavender across the sheet saying: "Soothing herb, smooth away our sorrows, bringing better tomorrows." Scatter most of the rose petals on the bed saying: "Delicate rose your scent shall help us to express our love as we repose." Place the rosemary on the pillows saying: "This rosemary shall dispel our stress and lay bare memories of our true tenderness." Put on a robe.

To the bathroom. Set out the candles safely. Light them as your partner returns home and fill the bath. When it's full add the oils and the rest of the rose petals and lavender.

Undress your partner, then both of you hop into the bath. A little bit of head and shoulder massage wouldn't go amiss. Focus the conversation on your partner. Avoid issues like bills, moving home or the baby's vaccinations.

When you both begin to feel revitalised, move to the bedroom. Light the candles, climb into bed and allow nature to take its course.

Once sated, allow your partner to sleep. Before you pass out, touch their face gently saying: "May we always find magic in a tender caress, kind words and simple togetherness."

Rose love spell

A long-term project to bring beauty and love, in all its guises, into your life. This spell also makes an excellent wedding gift.

The precise treatment of roses depends on the the variety you choose. But generally, prune back two thirds of last year's growth in the dormant period.

pot with fertile, moist but well-drained soil and display in a sunny site (outside).

Place the shells on the soil, saying, "Come fire and air, come water and earth, together with Akasha, Spirit of the universe. By your presence this rose will grow and by her blooms may love grow

a miniature rose • 5 seashells • time and attention

Cut back dead wood entirely. Feed occasionally in the winter with a balanced organic plant food and mulch. In spring and summer feed at three-weekly intervals.

Choose a slightly fragrant species (none of the miniatures seems to have a whopping scent) such as Pink Sunblaze or Hula Girl. (Pink represents Venus and is the colour of love and friendship.) Plant in a

also within the hearts of those with the sense to sense and know."

Miniature rose bushes are remontant, meaning if you remove spent blooms, others will grow to replace them. But you might as well cut them when the blooms are fresh. Seven rose buds may be strewn in the bath prior to an important date or sewn, along with lavender, in two squares of muslin to hang above your bed.

Tonight is the night

You've met an attractive specimen. He or she gives great date and you'd like to investigate further. This spell should ensure that your first physical encounter is a happy one.

available to me.
God, Goddess, Spirit,
If that is who you be,
If it be your will, then so will it be
That I spend a sensual

an oil burner • an orange candle • a hair from his/her head (snaffled on your last meeting) • a hair from your own head • 3 drops of bergamot or geranium oil

After an invigorating shower, pour 5 drops of neroli oil on the burner. Light the candle. Sit cross-legged on the floor in front of it, hands resting, palms upwards, on your knees.

Breathe in through your nose and out through your mouth seven times (see page 13). Feel the stresses and strains of the day falling away from your mind and body.

Say out loud:
"I call on the powers

magical night
with he (or she)."

Before going out extinguish the candle (don't forget there's one under the burner).

When you arrive home, light the candle again and the oil burner which may be topped up with warm water before adding a drop more oil. The rest is up to you. Both of you.

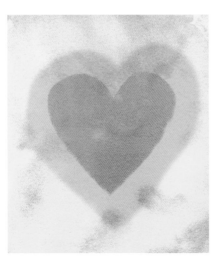

Nymph syndrome

Sex without love is like bread without butter. It's okay but it don't taste so great. And just because you have bread in your larder, it doesn't automatically mean that you have butter in your fridge. They are two separate things that just happen to go well together.

If you can't manage the ideal of love with sex, you should opt for love with no sex, rather than the reverse. But sex is practically a currency these days. We trade it for company, warmth and to dispel boredom.

For those of you who chase orgasms like addicts looking to score a fix, do I need to spell out the health risks? AIDS is the most obvious concern. Then there's gonorrhoea (often symptomless, but it plays havoc with the fallopian tubes), syphilis, and the lack of respect your behaviour affords you. Not to mention the other risks you take, making off with strangers all the time.

To take your mind off your obsession, take up gardening, horse riding or both.

a cold shower • a loofah
• 10ml of sweet almond oil mixed with 5 drops of marjoram oil

Try any spell in this book that will help you to see the reality of your situation and use this one – as often as you like.

Get into the shower, cool yourself off, pour the oil mixture on to your loofah and scrub yourself all over.

You may also benefit from regular doses of chamomile tea, infused with a sprig of marjoram. Now keep your legs together and get on with healing your life.

SPELLS FOR CAREERS

The difference between a career and a job is that the former is enjoyable and expresses your personal talents, while the latter is something we do in order to earn money to survive. Having said that, working in a job can be a happy activity while a career can get you down at times, especially when you're trying to balance it with family demands.

Balance, as usual is the key. The following spells are designed to help you to get the most out of whatever you do for a living and provide opportunities for change where necessary.

Interview libation

A useful spell for anyone setting their career on the line across a table. However good you are at your work, you have to be able to sell yourself in an interview setting. This should help you to steady your nerves and focus your

Charge me with your energies that I may please those I seek to please."

Put the cup to your lips and drink (just a sip) saying: "This offering is for the Spirit."

Pour the wine around the circle

a cup of wine • a candle (in a glass or jar) • 7 pebbles

mind. Bear in mind, though, that some jobs you won't get and it's usually for the best.

Outside at sunrise on the day of the interview, place the pebbles in a circle and place the candle (alight) within it. Lift the cup into the air, saying, "On this most auspicious day, I call upon the elements and the fifth essence, Spirit.

between the stones and the candle saying: "I can succeed, I will succeed if it be our will, and it uphold the rede."

Don't forget to clean your teeth or suck a mint – you don't want to arrive smelling of alcohol. Explaining to prospective employers that you have in fact simply been casting a spell may not be helpful.

Career change

At certain times of our lives we need a change of direction. Maybe an exhausting commute is draining your life blood, or you're unhappy with an employer's unfriendly attitude towards the family.

Or perhaps you've simply come round to the idea of downshifting, a movement

choices you will have covered some of the ground needed to make an important career decision.

Which of the following best describes you?

1) I have a good idea about what I'd like to do, but sometimes it's easier to just carry on as normal in my safe rut. If

in addition to the appropriately coloured candle (see below), you will also need a sage stick • a small amulet (a tiny metal of glass bottle, or securely fastening locket • a heat-proof bowl • a pen • paper

that's been gaining in popularity since the 1970s. Those who have gone for it realise that a large wage isn't everything and they opt to work part-time or from home, earning less but saving time, money and energy while pursuing a career that actively interests them as well as enjoying a better quality of life.

If you'd prefer to avoid downshifting and move your career up a gear instead, an improved life quality should still be your aim. Otherwise, what's the point?

For this spell you need to choose your own ingredients because by making your

only I could be braver and go for it.

2) I tend to jump before I look. A bit more forethought wouldn't go amiss. I want to avoid a disastrous error of judgment.

3) I don't know what I want. But something has to change, otherwise years will pass and I'll look back and think: "What was the point?"

4) I want to make a living from my hobby. I think I'm good enough and so do my friends. But it's such a risk since I'm worried I don't have the skills needed to sell myself.

Having identified your own thoughts choose the appropriate oil and candle colour from the list below.:

1) **geranium oil, dark purple candle**
2) **lavender oil, dark blue candle**
3) **bergamot oil, lilac candle**
4) **jonquil oil, yellow candle**

Light the sage and waft it around the room, saying, "I cleanse this space to prepare for change. May my decisions be wise and may I act upon my thoughts."

Heat your oil in a burner. Light your candle and place it on a table in front of you (turn off all other lights in the room). Sit on a hard-backed chair and begin the breathing exercise on page 13.

On the in-breath, breathe in golden success and on out breaths, breathe out dark negativity. Ask yourself the following questions. If you don't know the answer, move on to the next before returning to the problematical questions.

What do I want to change (don't just say your job. It's more about what aspects of your life you want to change)?

What do I want to remain the same?

What would realistically allow me to achieve these goals?

How could I make these changes?

What is likely to stop me?

Take as long as you like. Keep breathing all the time.

When you have made your decisions, write them down on the paper, fold it and place beneath the candle.

Continue to meditate on your answers and when you are ready say, "I have made some valuable life choices. I will change my life for the better. In moments of weakness I shall seek help from the Spirit abundant in all things. If I look I shall find and be helped."

Take the paper and burn it by the candle (have your heat-proof bowl ready to catch the ashes).

Place the ashes in the amulet, which may be worn around your neck or kept somewhere about your person. This will act as a reminder of your resolutions and what stands in your way. If it is a person who is likely to stop you, you will have to discuss the issues sensitively with them.

The horrid boss

Nasty employers expect the earth but the word "please" is a stranger to their pinched lips. They shouldn't be allowed to keep pets, let alone employ fellow human beings.

The best solution is to fire them. Yes, that's right, fire them. Find a more

If there is no possibility of immediate escape, remembering the witches' law (whatever magic you send out, comes back to you by the power of three), here's a spell that sails close enough to the wind for you to feel avenged, while not specifically wishing the offender any

3 red chilli peppers
• a piece of ginger • a white ribbon • 3 pins • a piece of
stationery belonging to your boss

appreciative outlet for your talents. There are plenty of friendly bosses and managers out there, who would never demand anything of anyone unless they were prepared to do it themselves. They have confidence in their own abilities and don't feel the need to belittle others.

They will also give you the odd day off to deal with your personal life.

But changing jobs right now may not be the best solution. You might be applying for a mortgage or perhaps plotting a promotion over the head of the hateful superior. (If that's your game, there's a helpful spell on page 106.)

harm. Any come-uppance is self-inflicted. They are making their own bad luck.

Arrive at work early. Before your boss arrives, sneak over and sit at their desk. Hold the peppers in your left hand and the ginger in your right while chanting:

"Your cruelty leaves you lacking friends.

You're neither clever, big or nice.
Your reign of terror now must end
I'll drain you with my mix of spice.
Want to save your precious career?
Then mend your ways.
The change starts here."

Visualise their nastiness being absorbed into the chilli and ginger. Pin the peppers to the ginger, wrap in the paper and bind with the white ribbon, chanting:

"This ribbon binds you to my will. You will change and I will too.

Store the package somewhere warm such as an airing cupboard for three days. Open it up and slice the chilli and ginger in half. Make sure all the pins are in the same half. Wrap this up again repeating both chants.

Deposit the parcel at the bottom of your employer's filing cabinet, or a suitable cupboard. Each time your boss is near it, draw strength from your inside knowledge and stand up for yourself – politely, of course. You may come to discover that your boss is an awful person because they are deeply unhappy about something (your imminent promotion over their head, perhaps).

Use the remaining chilli and ginger in a noodle dish. As you eat, imagine that you are devouring the less savoury aspects of their personality. Have a large glass of wine with your meal – a symbolic antidote to prevent you picking up those bad habits.

Heading for the top

The best way to secure a promotion is to be the best at what you do, as well as being a lovely person to have around. You must understand the subtleties of man-management and the personal needs of workers and never be afraid of responsibilities.

Lower your leg to the ground and repeat with the other leg. Do this seven times with each leg. Breathe deeply in through your nose and out through your mouth. Say to yourself, or out loud between breaths, "I am destined for this job. I'm the right person. I have the

a yellow candle • a green candle • a purple candle • 2 drops of rosemary oil • 2 drops of eucalyptus oil • a drop of black pepper oil • oil burner • a mirror

Do you still want your boss's job? If you do, this spell may help you to focus. But it will have little control over your competition.

Rise early each day. At sunrise, after an invigorating shower, light your candles and heat your oil.

Facing the mirror, hold your arms out in a V and lift one leg up in front of you. Keeping your balance, keep the leg raised and carry it around to behind you (don't strain yourself – this is a form of tai-chi, not the New York City Ballet).

credentials. I will be humble but I will be determined. I can succeed, I will succeed."

Carry this thought with you through your working day. I wish you success. Don't forget to blow your candles out before you leave home, will you? Including the one under the burner.

This spell may equally be performed outdoors. Instead of using the oils, candles and the mirror, focus on the sky, the horizon or your surroundings.

SPELLS FOR WEALTH

Measuring wealth in terms of health and friendship provides a better assessment of happiness than counting coins. But since money worries can wreak havoc on health and relationships, here are some money spells. None of them will help you to win the lottery or attract an unexpected windfall. Spells cast for financial gain may "gain" more than you bargained for. What comfort is money when it comes in the form of a life insurance payout at the death of a loved one? You might try to shrug off such events as "coincidence", but you'll never be sure and the guilt will eat away at your spirit.

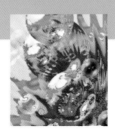

Financial strategy

How healthy is your bank account? Are your credit cards running on empty? Exceeded your overdraft limit and crippled with penalty charges?

As usual the problem must be approached logically as well as magically. If you've just received an ugly letter, first go outside and kick a wall. Take a few deep breaths and come back in.

Now write down all your outgoings on a sheet of paper. On another, write down all monies coming in. Compare the totals on each. Ideally your outgoings will be less than your incomings. If not, make sacrifices. (Taking your bank manager off to a natural altar in the woods for some blood-letting is an interesting idea, but totally against the witches' rede.)

You need to sacrifice something personal to you. Be realistic, reasonable and kind. You may well decide, after some soul-searching, that you want to continue filling your home with fresh flowers every week. In which case, chrysanthemums are relatively cheap and last longer than most. So there's a compromise.

Perhaps you could buy less expensive junk food and make an effort to cook more. It's far cheaper and better for you. Or wear out the shoes you have before adding to your collection.

When you have resolved to make changes, cast the destiny spell on page 44. The following three spells may also prove useful.

I hate my bank manager

"I was just following orders," has been used down the centuries to justify a multitude of terrible sins. No doubt, your average bank manager would subscribe to this excuse as he squeezes your small business into oblivion or practically puts you under house arrest by freezing your overdraft limit and credit cards.

You may well hate him or her for being callous and unhelpful. But you're only charged for borrowing when you borrow. Would you rather they allow you to sink further and further into debt? No. So get your hatred out, before

the chair or cushion is the bank manager and show him or her exactly what you think of them. Go on, let it out. Don't be afraid to yell.

When you come through the other side of this highly cathartic experience, sit up straight on a chair or cushion (if the chair's no longer in one piece fetch another) and follow the breathing exercise on page 13.

When the breathing has dispelled any remaining anger and you begin to feel more relaxed, light the white candles one by one saying: "The time has come

5 black candles • patchouli oil • oil burner • a big stick • an old chair or large cushion • 5 white candles • paper and pen

attempting to rationalise your financial situation in a calmer frame of mind. Whatever you do, don't stop communicating with your bank. You never know, they may be overcharging you, making mistakes which could lead to repayment or compensation even.

Light the black candles and warm the oil on a burner. Pick up the stick, pretend

to face my dilemma, calmly and honestly. May the God and Goddess bless me and relieve me of my stress. May the Spirit give me strength to resolve this mess."

Sit down with a blank piece of paper and come up with five ideas to ease your financial burden that won't harm others or yourself. Pin it up on the wall and follow your own instructions.

The credit card spell

This one is an absolute winner.

Light a bonfire either in your garden or a friend's if you don't have one of your own.

Keep up the chant and begin to move faster and faster. When you're suitably fired up throw the cards on to the flames. Go on, do it. Then chant,

a bonfire • a hazel stang or wand
• your credit cards (you may keep one for genuine emergencies)

Walk around it in a clockwise direction, pointing towards the flame with your wand or stang, holding the cards in your left hand. As you do, chant, "I can change, I will change. There's more to life than this. I'll find a way to live in peace in solvency and bliss."

"Goodbye cards, I won't miss you and you will not miss me. Now you've gone I'm better off, I'm free I'm free I'm free."

Now you just have to pay off the debts. Chip away every month paying more than just the interest due.

Dodgy salesmen

Prior to viewing a car or a potential new home, or when salesmen call round or contact you by phone, this extremely simple gesture may protect you from slick techniques aimed at luring you actually refuse to sell it to you. In the same way, this is also a useful spell for shopping addicts to cast before entering a department store.

Trace a pentagram with your hand in

your hands • belief

into parting with your money. Sometimes this spell is so successful, even when you fall in love with a totally impractical banger (because it has a nice fender) or a run-down "character home with potential", the vendor will front of you. Visualise it, actually see it. Remember it's there as you walk around the showroom or shop, or find yourself about to offer the vacuum cleaner salesmen yet another cup of coffee.

Happiness growing spell

The Romans used to throw coins on to farmland as a gift to the God Ceres. That's why old Roman coins are often still turned up by the plough. Now I'm not saying that planting money actually causes money or corn to grow. But I do believe that to reap rewards we need to make sacrifices of the personal rather than the goat or virgin variety. You must commit totally to improving your situation.

This spell is particularly helpful when cast in conjunction with the credit card spell.

On the pot, using the gold paint or ink, paint the symbols for magical energy, blessings and fertility.

Place crock in the bottom, then some earth and the coins before adding the plant and filling in with earth around the edges. Say, "May Akasha bless me with good fortune and may that fortune grow and may I never abuse this chance to end my woe."

Keep the plant on a sunny windowsill if you can. A week prior to a full moon, place a crystal on the soil saying: "Bless me God, bless me goddess, bless me with growing happiness."

The day after the full moon, put the crystal in your purse. Carry it with you as a reminder of what you are trying to achieve (you'll be amazed how adept we are at double think. We know we have no money, but it doesn't stop us spending what we don't have).

A week prior to the next full moon, place the crystal on the soil again for an energising top-up. Then it's back into your purse.

> **a jade plant or a cutting from one (if a friend has a good-sized plant they should happily part with a stem) • a suitable-sized pot (just a little bigger than the pot it comes in or a reasonable size for the cutting) • gold paint or ink • 3 coins • a crystal**

Once you become aware of a growing sense of happiness – it may take about three months – pass on the crystal and the spell to someone deserving who will carry it through. Spreading happiness breeds happiness.

Giving spell

As the gap between the rich and poor widens, a new syndrome has cropped up among the wealthy: affluenza. Basically, this depressing condition

Run through your mind all sorts of issues that don't really affect you but you know to be important to those less "fortunate" than yourself. Narrow the

a bath • 3 drops of rose oil • 3 drops of chamomile oil • 3 drops of jasmine oil

renders the victim unable to see much point to life, caused by the dawning realisation that money cannot buy happiness.

"Give me the chance to prove it," some might say. But if you are hideously rich or comfortably well off (symptoms include a bulging bank account, a fleet of homes and an overflowing wardrobe of designer clothes), this spell is for you.

Fill a bath, pour in the drops and swish around. Lie back, allow this luxurious treat to envelope you as close your eyes. Begin your breathing (see page 13).

field down to five concerns which are supported by charitable organisations. One should involve animals and one the environment. The other three should focus on humanitarian needs.

When you have decided upon five concerns that capture your imagination write out big fat cheques to each and send them off anonymously to the local branch of your chosen charities (money tends to be "absorbed" when sent to a head office). You'll make a lot of people's day, and make your own to boot.

This spell can be repeated as often as necessary.

Pay me please

Late payment can play havoc with your cash flow. If you've invoiced, re-invoiced and harassed by phone and there's still no sign of a cheque, my mother advises that you borrow two small children (if you don't have any of your own), turn up at the company's office, give the kids chocolate and let them run riot until the finance director sees sense and writes that cheque. This dramatic course of action works equally well with all manner of bureaucratic misdemeanours.

In the meantime try this.

Light the candle and begin your breathing (see page 13).

Say, "I call on the Spirit to lend its force in my great time of need. Protect me from those who selfishly harm me by their greed. Encourage them to act with speed, and send a cheque to me. If it be the Spirit's will, then so will it be."

Envisage the debtor writing out a cheque and posting it to you. Imagine it arriving at your door and you paying it into your bank account.

Pick up the invoice, light it from the candle and drop it into the bowl. As you watch it burn say: "It will be, it will be, it will be."

If the company goes into liquidation leaving you unpaid, try the Forgiving the unforgivable spell (see page 83) and the Happiness growing spell (page 114).

a green candle
- **a copy (not the original) of the invoice with the word "paid" written across it**
- **a heat-proof bowl**

Humbleness spell

Don't insist on picking up the tab in a restaurant to give friends the impression you're doing better than you are. Don't attempt a building job if you have no idea what you're doing and it's going to cost you squillions to pay someone else to put it right. Don't run a car you can't afford. Don't opt for the most expensive anything just to show off to the shop assistant (even if she did treat you like dirt when you arrived).

Do cast this simple spell, to stop this pride business eating away at your overdraft.

Huge rocks called geodes are guaranteed to humble if you have enough disposable income.

Sit cross-legged on the floor in front of your crystal and worship it. Admire

the largest amethyst crystal you can truly afford

the beauty, the shape, the colours. Feel its energy through your hands.

Say to yourself, "May the crystal soothe my swollen ego. Banish my bane and let the real me remain. Let me feel pride where pride is due, and humbleness, long overdue."

SPELLS
FOR
PRACTICAL
MAGIC

The following spells are easy to do

and rely on the efficacy of natural

ingredients as much as on the

potency of your mind to harness

magical energies. They also require

practical skills which will improve

with practice.

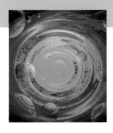

Tussie mussie

Made from a single red rose and herbs, a tussie mussie represents a meaningful wedding bouquet, a healing gift or a celebration of friendship.

The herbs used will depend on the season. In the autumn and winter your

chamomile, fennel, chive flowers, basil and mint.

Trim your rose and herb stems to about 17.5cm/7in long. Surround the rose with a ring of one herb at a time to form concentric circles. On the outside,

a rose, chosen for its suitably symbolic colour (see chart on page 25)
• a choice of herbs according to availability • pale blue ribbon
• 7 round leaves, depending on what's in season

choice will be more limited. But rosemary, lavender foliage, thyme and sage are still available and should be included all year round. From your indoor plants you have mint and lemon scented varieties of pelargoniums. In summer, you may add lavender flowers, lemon balm, lemon verbena (vervain),

wrap with leaves. Bind with the ribbon, saying, "May these herbs, blessed by the sun, nurtured by the air, the water and the earth, bring love, harmony, happiness, peace and mirth."

The tussie mussie should be kept in a small vase and the water changed every day.

My mother's bread spell

Successful people enjoy a challenge. There's more satisfaction to be derived from achieving against the odds, especially when it involves determination and effort. The easy way out never has the same kick.

Buying bread is easy. Baking your own will expand your horizons, helping you to fully realise that going the extra mile has its own rewards.

You have to use your loaf when bread baking. The kind of yeast, sugar and flour used will affect texture and size. The temperature of your oven is also important and chances are this won't tally with the numbers on the dial. Weights are only estimates. Getting it right may depend on anything from the

Place the dough in a warm, oiled bowl, cover with cling film and a tea towel and leave somewhere with an even warm (not hot) temperature until it has doubled in size.

Knock the dough back by giving it a mega thump to get rid of the air, then allow it to rise again. Cut off a third and shape into rolls. Put the rest in an oiled and floured bread tin. Cover with cling

About 750/1lb of wholemeal flour • a generous teaspoon salt • a pinch of brown sugar • about 400ml/³/₄ pint warm water • 2 teaspoons fresh yeast (or dried yeast of your choice)

flour to the weather. Trial and error, as with all spells, is the key. Happy baking.

Dissolve the yeast in half a cup of the warm water, add the sugar and leave to froth. Put the flour in a warm bowl, make a well in the middle and pour in the yeast mixture, followed by the rest of the water.

Gradually stir it all together with a knife to form a scone-like dough. Knead for as long as it takes for the dough to become smooth and elastic. If it's sticky, add more flour (you can always use more flour but never use more yeast).

film and allow to prove (rise again). The dough is very sensitive to draughts at this point, so take care.

When the dough fills the tin, bake at 220°C (450°F, gas 7–8) for the first 10-15 minutes and then reduce to 200°C (400°F gas 6–7) for the rest of the baking time (a total of 30–35 minutes for rolls, 40–45 for loaves).

When removed from the tins and tapped underneath the loaves will give a hollow ring, rather than a thud. Always cool bread on wire racks or the condensed steam will make it heavy.

Serve with cheeses and friends.

Technology amulet (tree spell)

Technology is supposed to help us. When it goes wrong, like when the car won't start, the computer screen freezes or the heating breaks down it can impact on our lives both physically and emotionally.

Evergreen or deciduous? Good spring blossoms or great autumn colour?

Rowan, birch, apple, hazel, hawthorn and gingko (eaten by the dinosaurs, positively ancient) all have something to offer your witch, as does oak, if you have

a tree • a crystal

To cope with such annoyances, plant a tree. That way, when chaos reigns you will have something to hug that will earth your anger and frustration while also cheering your spirits.

Choose your tree carefully in line with good old-fashioned gardening sense. You want a specimen that will positively thrive in your local soil and climate conditions. Also think about position – where you plan to plant your tree – considering the potential height and rooting habit (roots can play havoc with foundations, especially in clay soils where subsidence is a problem). Aesthetics also count: do you prefer tall and slender? Short and chunky?

a big enough garden.

Buy your tree from an established specialist nursery rather than a garden centre. Plant it at the correct time of year and follow the instructions for tending it carefully.

Plant your tree, placing a crystal under the root ball. When the job is complete say, "Symbol of Spirit, emblem of life keeper of wisdom far greater than mine. I promise to tend your every need, respecting, nurturing and protecting you. All I ask is that when needs be in return for a hug you shall comfort me."

Whenever the going gets tough, get out there and hug away. Trees love it and so do witches.

Stargazing

A difficult spell for urban witches since the light pollution makes it difficult to see many stars. Stargazing is best done in the open countryside. Even if you don't know the names of the constellations, stargazing is an absorbing, inspirational focus on the darkness, you may begin to see stars even further away. As you look, dwell on these facts.

There are an estimated 100,000 million stars in our galaxy alone. Called the Milky Way, it is spiral-shaped. The

something waterproof to lie on • a cushion or pillow for your head • sensible clothing • possibly a sleeping bag

activity guaranteed to fill you with awe, if you think about what you are looking at. It can also help to put your life and your very existence into some sort of perspective.

Stare up at the stars then at the gaps between the stars. When your eyes nearest star to us, other than our own sun, is four light years away. There aren't many more within a 10-light-year radius.

It is believed that the universe began around 15,000 million years ago. We have no idea how or why. We may never know. . . .

Cloud games

Ideal for entertaining children on long journeys or just in your back garden.

Look up at the clouds and describe what you see. Castles in the air?

some clouds • some imagination

Adults will also enjoy it if they give themselves permission. This "exercise" helps to develop imagination and visualisation skills, as well as bringing you closer to the Spirit.

Dragons? Your great aunt's nose? When playing this game with others, it's interesting to see what shapes you interpret the same – and which you don't.

Express the rhythm

The rhythm of life is a powerful beat, as the song goes. Learn to hear it, feel it and express it by signing up for a series of tap dancing classes or drumming workshops. Either will allow you to dig those rhythms.

and that these styles merged in America's big cities. The variety of the rhythms are thought to reflect the sounds of urban life, from traffic snarl-ups to building sites.

If you can tap dance or drum, instead

tap shoes • drums • determination

No one can agree where tap dancing comes from. The most believable theory is that it has its roots in the dances of Africa, Ireland and Britain's Morris Men,

of getting angry next time you're the victim of noise pollution, you can join in or dance to the sounds instead. Not only that, but drumming or tapping is an international language – you will make friends wherever you go, communicating without ever having to utter a word.

Act of kindness

A version of this spell appeared in my first book *Spells for Teenage Witches*. The hope is that if everyone does this, two things will be achieved: inner peace, and from that will come world peace. For this, we need all the adults to join in. The source of this spell is from one of the wisest men alive at the time of writing, His Holiness, the Dalai Lama of Tibet.

Light the candle in a darkened room and begin your breathing (see page 13). Gaze into the flame's aura, the light that emanates from the flame. Dwell on the Dalai Lama's words, "The key point is kindness. With kindness one will have inner peace. Through inner peace, world peace can one day be a reality."

The following day go out of your way to be kind to someone. They may be a stranger or someone at work or at the shops who you wouldn't normally engage in conversation, let alone offer to help. Through talking you will discover their need.

an orange candle

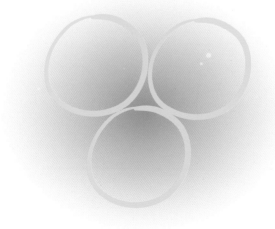

TV spell

Watching too much television? Probably. This spell will help you to make up your own mind. If you decide you are

an amethyst crystal • a clock

overdoing it, replace this unhealthy habit with a helpful hobby such as gardening, bread baking or exercise.

Hold the crystal in your hand as you watch television. From time to time, you will remember you're holding it. Look at the clock. Continue to watch if your conscience allows. Next time you feel the rock in your hand, check the clock again. How long have you been stuck there now?

When you can stand it no longer, go and do something less boring instead.

Washing Up Spell

This saves on the number of dirty saucepans hanging around, which are certainly the bane of my life. You will still

a cauldron • oil • organic meat if required • a selection of organic vegetables • stock • basically anything in your fridge that needs eating up. If you have cooked vegetables, pop them in for the last few minutes.

need plates, unless eating alone or you hand round spoons and encourage dinner guests simply to tuck in. The humble fondue is a good alternative to this recipe, if you like cheese.

On an open fire or on a stove, heat the oil in the cauldron, add the meat first, browning the outside then add the vegetables. When they begin to soften, add the stock and simmer until cooked, stirring occasionally.

Serve with homemade bread and friends, who should be asked to wash their own bowl and cutlery afterwards.

To clean the cauldron, add a chopped stick of rhubarb to a few pints of water and boil. Even the most stubborn burned potato at the bottom will lift off in minutes. Easy peasy.

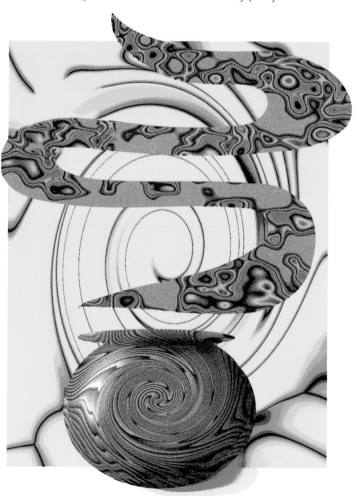

Co-ordination spell

As much as 7 per cent of the population suffers from dyspraxia. Symptoms manifest as, among other things, apparent clumsiness. Those affected find throwing and catching a mystery. They might also experience speech difficulties – they know what they want to say but can't quite get the words out.

symptom of manhood (coincidentally dyspraxia affects four times as many men as women). Yet some male specimens are perfectly capable of cooking, while minding the children, cleaning the house and pouring you a drink. These supermen are admittedly rare, but they do exist.

a bowl • 7 pebbles (or small crystals, a mixture is fine)
• a handful of basil leaves • 3 sprigs of rosemary
• a handful of peppermint leaves • rosemary oil

Serious cases are usually diagnosed in childhood. But you could easily reach adulthood without realising the underlying cause of your apparent lack of grace. It is never too late seek help. If you think you might be dyspraxic talk to your doctor. They may refer you to an occupational therapist who can help you to overcome your difficulties.

But there are plenty of us who don't suffer from dyspraxia and yet find it almost impossible to do more than one thing at a time. Many friends insist it's a common

Many women, on the other hand, might well panic when opening a letter – if the phone rings, the doorbell goes and a child demands attention simultaneously.

So let's put aside gender issues and agree that we could all benefit from a spell promoting mental and physical order to enhance our multi-tasking skills.

Place all the ingredients in a bowl (except the oil) and stir vigorously with your right or left hand (depending on whether you are left- or right-handed). You should

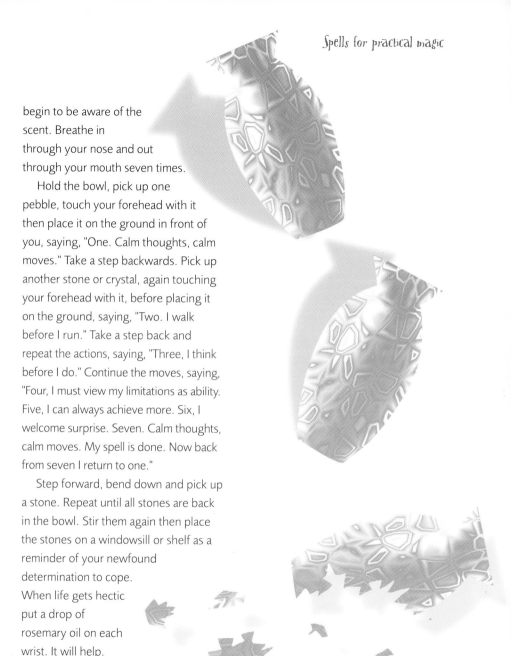

begin to be aware of the
scent. Breathe in
through your nose and out
through your mouth seven times.

Hold the bowl, pick up one
pebble, touch your forehead with it
then place it on the ground in front of
you, saying, "One. Calm thoughts, calm
moves." Take a step backwards. Pick up
another stone or crystal, again touching
your forehead with it, before placing it
on the ground, saying, "Two. I walk
before I run." Take a step back and
repeat the actions, saying, "Three, I think
before I do." Continue the moves, saying,
"Four, I must view my limitations as ability.
Five, I can always achieve more. Six, I
welcome surprise. Seven. Calm thoughts,
calm moves. My spell is done. Now back
from seven I return to one."

Step forward, bend down and pick up
a stone. Repeat until all stones are back
in the bowl. Stir them again then place
the stones on a windowsill or shelf as a
reminder of your newfound
determination to cope.
When life gets hectic
put a drop of
rosemary oil on each
wrist. It will help.

A basket case

Only the pathologically untidy know how difficult life can be when you continually have to step over and around piles of "things." They must be shifted before you can sit down, moved before you can eat and scattered to open wardrobes.

Witches are actually untidy creatures

how you'd like it. Now imagine it again with half the stuff. That's what you're aiming to achieve.

Say to yourself, "This is it, I'm going to do what is long overdue. Tidy away and make my day. Spirit give me strength and light my way and allow these

3 large willow baskets • bergamot oil • half a packet of salt • a few handfuls of lavender

by nature and do their best to help those with housework fixations hoping to inspire them with homely surrounds or get their home tidied for free. But when you can't open your front door without an inevitable upheaval it's time for a spell.

Tempting as it is to stuff the baskets with the nearest debris to hand and hide them under the bed (if there's room), this is not the idea.

Begin this spell in just one untidy room. Heat the oil in a burner. Sit with your baskets in front of you and breathe. Imagine the room, free from clutter, just

baskets to magic this mess away."

Starting from the floor, working up to your top shelves, make three piles, all containing things that you definitely wish to keep (leave the rest in situ for now). These could consist of paperwork, clothes and toys, or one could be miscellaneous items that live elsewhere in your home.

As the piles increase in size, put each one in a basket. Now off you go and put it all away.

When you've exhausted the "must keep" objects, begin three new piles. One consists of rubbish, the second is charity shop goods and the third is "don't know".

Keep going until you've run out things for the bin and the charity shop. Empty those into bin liners, but don't confuse the bags.

You will now have two empty baskets and either a pile or a basket full of don't knows. Sort through these items, deal with what you wish to be rid of and you should be left with one last basket of stuff to put away. If the cupboards are full, use the basket routine here as well.

Eventually you will be left with three empty baskets and a tidy room. Move on to the next bomb site and repeat.

Once a room is tidied and wiped clean (see the helpful potion on page 90), sprinkle salt and lavender on the carpet and leave over night. The following day vacuum it up. On the next new moon try the Resolution spell (see page 42) and persuade yourself to make a bit more of an effort to be tidy in future.

THE
SABBATS

The Sabbats are our most enduring rites, having been celebrated since the Bronze Age and before. A sophisticated knowledge of the night sky allowed the Druids (the political and spiritual leaders of the Celts) to predict the changing seasons and plot specific dates, using the position of the moon and other heavenly bodies.

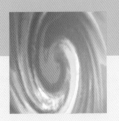

This ability allowed people to plan their lives. Time-keeping gave them power over their present and future as well as the chance to co-operate with nature. Around the times of the sabbats the people would gather at sacred sites where they would worship, offering thanks and sacrifices to the deities. They would also trade material goods between each other, catch up with their news, welcome new arrivals, meet new people and expand the gene pool.

In short sabbats worked on every level, giving meaning to life while actively promoting it.

Lessons learned by the ancestors could be reinforced in the present and preserved, to be handed down to future generations through story-telling and ritual.

These lessons are just as relevant today. By celebrating the sabbats we acknowledge the turning wheel of the year and the changes this brings. It also helps us to come to terms with our own mortality as we can view our existence as part of the pattern of life.

View days as a cycle (although the Druids counted nights rather than days), months as another cycle, and the year as a third and you begin to have a structured framework for your future, instead of one long drawn out line of time, on which you may or may not notch up successes and life-defining moments: a daunting prospect on the best of days.

To get the most out of your sabbats, read up on the subject elsewhere (see Further Reading, page 143) and I would suggest that building a fire is an absolute must since it offers ritual cleansing, a focus and warmth. If this is not possible, go for as many candles as you can safely accommodate.

Samhain 31st October

Now known as Halloween, samhain celebrants acknowledge this as the first day of the year, a time to prepare the ground so that it will be at its optimum fertility in the spring.

Sahaim also, therefore, marks the dying of the old year, and is a time to remember loved ones who are no longer with us.

ambience

seasonal flowers such as
   chrysanthemums, orange and red
   if possible
orange candles
carved pumpkins
burn rosemary branches on your fire

catering

bowls of fruit and nuts
pumpkin soup garnished with rosemary
   (served in a pumpkin cauldron)
homemade bread
cheeses
bake biscuits and decorate with spirals or
   pentacles for children who come trick
   or treating

suggested rituals

In a window light seven candles in memory of family and friends who have passed on.

Take a few moments to remember and respect them, giving thanks for their lives.

Invite a psychic to your home to give 15-minute readings to your friends as they arrive. Explain this is the time of year to take stock and to make resolutions for the future.

Give each friend a bay leaf. Let them dwell on something they'd like to put behind them before throwing it – along with their problem (so long as it's not another person) on to the fire.

It is traditional only on this day to dance around your bonfire in an anti-clockwise direction. At all other sabbats and when casting spells, dance around clockwise.

Dancing around bonfires doesn't just allow your witch to flourish, it means everyone gets a turn – just a brief one – standing downwind and in the path of the smoke.

Yule 21st December

The longest night, the shortest day, marking the return journey from winter back to spring and summer. This celebration marks the rebirth of light and is fast becoming as popular as – if not more so than – Christmas (which borrowed many of Yule's more ancient traditions), since it is deemed more relevant than the story of the nativity, or the tale of Santa Claus.

ambience

Deck the halls with holly and other greenery. Red berries, such as hips, are also good. Children can make paper chains and snowflakes out of white paper.

Decorate a tree (fake, outdoors or potted with its root ball) with stars and moons (made from cardboard, biscuits, modelling clay or wood).

Use black candles symbolising light coming out of darkness, as well as red and green candles

Burn an oak log as a sacrifice to the forest. (Don't cut a tree down especially, please!)

catering

roasted organic meats and seasonal
  vegetables such as sprouts potatoes,
  broccoli and leeks
crystallised and dried fruits
chocolates

suggested rituals

Hand each guest a candle. Light one candle from your bonfire and pass light around. As you do, say, "We celebrate the rebirth of light."

Ask guests to make paper lanterns beforehand that may be lit with night lights. At the end of the evening throw these on to the fire as a sacrifice of light to light.

Imbolg 2nd February

Resurrection, rebirth after the dark months. The quickening of the earth, life stirring in the Great Mother's womb. The first spring flowers are showing and buds are visible on the trees. A goddess festival celebrating the three ages of womankind, the maid, the mother and the grandmother.

ambience

white flowers, white candles
burn apple logs (soaked in brine for a full moon cycle before being dried out)

catering

soup, homemade bread, fruit
flap jacks, egg dishes

suggested rituals

Each person takes it in turn to hold an apple log and think about his or her mother and grandmother, and their mothers and grandmothers who lived before. Give thanks for their lives which gave you your life. When everyone has had a go, place the log on the fire, saying, "For all our mothers we give thanks, Great Goddess. For their sacrifice and the gift of life."

Beltane 1st May

May Day, a time of growth, of coupling. Carefree, warm, the ground and trees have burst into life.

ambience
coloured ribbons,
green foliage

catering
early summer flowers
sandwiches
yoghurt
fruit

suggested rituals
Country dancing – around a maypole or tall tree such as a birch with ribbons tied from its branches.
Morris dancing
Women dress as May Queens, in pale coloured dresses with flowers in their hair. Men dress as the Green Man with green clothing and foliage head-dresses. This is also a great date for a hand-fasting ceremony, when two people commit themselves to living as a couple for a year and a day.

Midsummer 21st June

The sun is at its zenith. The wheel is turning and winter is returning. The longest day of the year.

ambience

rose and herb tussie mussies (see page 120)
yellow and light blue candles
outdoor flame torches

catering

freeze vervain flowers in ice cubes and serve with a chilled herbal infusion of lemon balm, mint and vervain.
fruit and herb sorbets
strawberries and cream
strawberry sandwiches
melon
salads
grilled meats

suggested rituals

Camp out under the stars.
Fill bowls with rose petals and floating candles and place either side of your

front door. As your guests enter, sprinkle water on their heads using sprigs of heather, saying, "You are blessed by God and Goddess. Be blessed."

Cook your meats on the fire. Burn basil leaves, to ward off flies and mosquitoes.

Lughnasa 31st July

The harvest is gathered in, a time to give thanks for the summer and to prepare for the autumn. It's a wild one. The hard toil of harvesting is over. It's like an exploding pressure cooker. Party like there's no tomorrow but do go slightly easy on yourselves. As Dorothy Parker explained in her poem "The Flaw in Paganism", "Drink and dance and laugh and lie, Love the reeling midnight through, For tomorrow we shall die! (But, alas, we never do)."

ambience

two bonfires

wheat sheaves

corn dollies

late summer blooms

lavender (home-grown and harvested around mid-August)

catering

home-made bread rolls

cheese

oatmeal cookies

bilberries

blackberries

Drink mead or cider.

Ask friends to bring a plate of food, preferably something they've grown and cooked themselves.

ritual suggestions

Dance on a hillside with friends.

Run between the bonfires for ritual cleansing.

Jump over the fires for similar reasons and to show you dare (not to be attempted when wearing flowing robes).

Lots of loud drumming to accompany the fire jumpers.

Useful addresses and further reading

From outside the UK, dial international + 44, and omit the first 0 of the number given here

Comfort and Joy
Toiletries and cosmetics for discerning witches. All natural, not tested on animals, hand made to order and delivered anywhere in the world. Good value, too.
Baytree Cottage, Eastlech, Nr Cirencester, Glos. GL7 3NL
01367 850278
Merri@comfortandjoy.co.uk

Rainbow Illuminations Ltd
Beautiful handcrafted pure beeswax candles. International mail order.
PO Box 468, Haywards Heath, West Sussex RH16 2YF.
01444 487 719

Fossil 2000
Simply the best Grade A crystals you'll find, every stone and rock individually cared for until the right person comes along...
3 Kensington Place, Brighton BN1 4EJ
01273 622000
fossil2000@hotmail.com

riverocean
Excellent lunar calendars and information regarding lunar festivals.
riverocean 113 Queens Road, Brighton, BN1 3XG
011273 234032
info@rore.org.uk
www.rore.org.uk

Further reading
Goddess and Green Man Bookshop
A great selection of Goddess and Pagan literature
2-4 High St, Glastonbury, Somerset BA6 9DU
01458 834697
goddess.shop@uk.com
www.goddessandgreenman.co.uk

Home birth
Sheila Kitzinger is a birth guru and goddess. No one should give birthwithout reading her books.
The New Pregnancy and Childbirth, Penguin,1997
Rediscovering Birth, Little, Brown, 2000.

Gardening
Bob Flowerdew's Organic Bible, Kyle Cathie, 1998, is a great book for beginners or experienced gardeners keen to change over to organic methods. Unpatronising but detailed.

Important organisations
Greenpeace International
An organisation dedicated to saving the world.
www.greenpeace.org/

Friends of the Earth International
Another fab organisation dedicated to making the world a better place.
www.foei.org/

Pagan Federation
For information about Pagan activities , and the magazine Pagan Dawn.
BM Box 7097, London WC1N 3XX
www.paganfed.org

Photographic acknowledgements: Clive Druett/Corbis: frog photograph; Tony Stone Images: pages 12/13 (David Sutherland), 107 (Ed Pritchard); NHPA: 21 (Laurie Campbell); Flowers & Foliage: 39; Still Pictures: 41 (Galen Rowell),123 (Vincent Decorde);Garden Picture Library: 43 (Christopher Gallagher); Sally Griffyn: 140/141

'The Flaw in Paganism' by Dorothy Parker, from The Collected Dorothy Parker, is reproduced by permission of Gerald Duckworth & Co. Ltd and Viking Penguin Inc., New York

Thanks also to Fossil 2000 of Brighton for the loan of crystals for photography.

Index